The D-Max Effect

Also By Lisa Liberatore

Power of Transparency
An Entrepreneur's Lessons on balancing it All

Power of Transparency:
Workbook for Navigating the Crisis Of 2020

D-Max's Birthday Wish
(By Dorian Pillsbury & Lisa Liberatore)

The D-Max Effect

What happens when a kid decides
to lead...and others follow?

Lisa Liberatore

TRANSPARENCY ENTERPRISES

This book reflects the author's personal experiences and perspectives. All organizations referenced are included for descriptive purposes only and do not imply endorsement. Any views expressed are solely those of the author.

Book Design: Edner Fago
Cover Photo: Lisa Liberatore
Back Cover Photo: Krystal Brouty

The Story Behind the Cover

Dorian was dropping off a load of donations when he noticed a wall covered in stickers - each one representing someone who had shown up, given back, or helped make a difference. He paused, looked at it, and said out loud, *"I want to be on that tree."* And then he went back to what he was doing. Dropping off items. Showing up. Giving back - without fanfare, without expectation.

A few months later, we got a call. Dorian had earned a sticker of his own.

When we returned, I watched him place it on the wall - carefully, deliberately - and then step back. The smile that spread across his face wasn't about recognition. It was about belonging. About realizing that his effort mattered. That he was part of something bigger than himself.

That moment was priceless.

This image captures what *The D-Max Effect* is really about: not spotlight moments, but the quiet joy that comes from choosing to show up and discovering, sometimes by surprise, that your choices have left a mark.

Acknowledgments

This book exists because of the people who showed me what it means to show up.

To my parents - thank you for raising me inside a community. You taught me, long before I had words for it, that service is a way of life, that consistency builds trust, and that how you treat people matters. Everything I know about leadership began with watching you.

To Dorian - thank you for inviting me on this adventure. Walking alongside you has reminded me that leadership can be joyful, curious, and deeply human. You didn't just inspire this book - you continue to teach me what's possible when we lead with heart.

To Scott - thank you for stepping in quietly and keeping everything moving forward. For your steadiness, your patience, and the countless unseen ways you support this life we're building. You are my safe place, my partner, and the love of my life.

And to you - yes, you.

The friend who shared a post. The neighbor who dropped off a donation. The teacher who stayed a little longer. The stranger who said yes without being asked twice. The quiet supporter who never needed credit and never stopped showing up.

You are not a footnote in this story. You are the reason it exists.

This book talks about what happens when people choose to see a child, believe in a community, and act - not someday, but now. You did that. Every time you showed up for Dorian, you were showing every child watching that they matter. That effort is contagious. That belonging is built, not found.

We didn't build *The D-Max Effect* alone. You built it with us.

So if this book found its way into your hands, know this: it was written with you in mind, it was made possible by your belief, and it belongs to you just as much as it belongs to us.

Thank you for being part of something bigger than any one of us.

Author's Notes

This book is for anyone who has ever felt the pull to create something meaningful even if you weren't quite sure what it would become.

It's for those who believe in connection, in shared purpose, and in the power of showing up, even when the path isn't clear. And it's for anyone who has felt the distance between the life they imagined-rich with trust, belonging, and community and the one they're still learning how to build. For me, that understanding didn't arrive all at once. It came into focus slowly: on a drive, through a conversation, one memory, one moment at a time. My son and I were invited to speak at Rotary. On the drive there, I told Dorian stories about my dad, about the years he spent in this very chapter, and the project that mattered most to him. Every winter, he ran the Salvation Army Angel Tree. I remember sitting in those meetings as a kid, helping collect gifts, watching adults quietly show up for families they might never meet. Standing at the podium decades later, I recognized so many familiar faces. My dad's friends. Fellow Rotarians. People who had shared a lifetime of service with him. And suddenly, the room felt heavy with what was missing. I felt it in my throat as I was wrapping up my comments and handing the microphone over to Dorian.

After Dorian spoke, someone raised their hand and said,

"Your grandfather would be so proud!" The response was immediate. Heads nodded. Eyes filled. The agreement was collective. Another member followed and said, *"After listening to this kid speak, we all can be doing so much more."*

During Dorian's talk, he showed a picture of himself with his grandpa at a lemonade stand they hosted together. Two generations sitting side by side with the biggest smiles on their faces. The room softened. Dorian beamed with pride-proud of his grandfather, proud of what he was carrying forward, proud to be standing there telling that story. At that moment, I saw something clearly: Community isn't something you inherit. It's something you choose.

Standing there, holding back tears, I could see more than grief in the room. I could see longing. The shared ache of missing someone. The recognition that legacy doesn't disappear-it moves, when someone is willing to carry it. Watching Dorian in that moment, I knew this hadn't happened by accident. It had been shaped by small, visible choices: inviting him into real conversations, letting him see effort instead of polish, modeling service before confidence, and choosing community even when it felt uncomfortable. Over time, those choices formed a pattern. What Dorian was learning wasn't just what to do-he was learning how to think.

This book is an exploration of a simple, lived truth: Children don't learn leadership by being told what it is-they learn it by being invited into it. I am deeply grateful to have been raised in a community. But if you weren't, if you've ever longed for a deeper sense of belonging, for real trust, real connection, and wondered why it hasn't come together the way you imagined-you've picked up the right book!

This book is about possibility. It's about how community is built intentionally, imperfectly, and over time. I'll show you how to begin, even if you're starting with nothing more than a willingness to try. This is not a manual. It's a journey. And being here means you've already begun.

Contents

Chapter 1:   The First Office I Ever Worked In.................................... 1

Chapter 2:   The House That Service Built.............................. 7

Chapter 3:   Breaking Cycles, Rewriting Futures..................... 15

Chapter 4:   Taco Tuesday....................................... 23

Chapter 5:   The Moment His Heart Became Visible To Others.......... 29

Chapter 6:   Raising A Heart-Led Leader While Rebuilding Yourself... 33

Chapter 7:   The First Fundraiser: The Spark That Lit Everything....... 41

Chapter 8:   Why consistency Is More Powerful Than Talent.............. 45

Chapter 9:   D-Max Merch & The Birth Of A Kid Entrepreneur........ 57

Chapter 10: The New Generational Wealth........................... 67

Chapter 11: Raising A Leader While Becoming One...................... 73

Chapter 12: What Happened When One Child Showed Up.............. 77

Chapter 13: When One Kid Moves, A Community Responds........... 81

Chapter 14: The Pause I Didn't Plan For............................ 87

Chapter 15: This Is Not His Story Or Mine - It's Ours.................... 93

Chapter 16: Learning It Together.................................. 99

Chapter 17: The Adults Who Said Yes........................... 105

Chapter 18: When Impact Becomes Tangible 109

Chapter 1

THE FIRST OFFICE
I EVER WORKED IN

Before I ever taught an entrepreneurship class…
Before I founded Lisa's Legit Burritos…
Before I published The Power of Transparency…
Before my son ever became "D-Max," the kid who believes he can end childhood hunger…I was a little girl standing behind a front desk in my dad's orthodontist office.

Most kids grew up separating "home" from "work." We didn't. Our life was one continuous circle of service. My dad fixed smiles. My mom ran the practice. Long before anyone named it, I learned my first leadership truth: education doesn't begin in a classroom. It begins at home-when someone trusts you with responsibility before you feel ready. Work wasn't a place we went. It was a mission our family shared. That office became my first classroom. At nine years old, I filed charts alphabetically the way my mom taught me, took payments from adults who trusted me with their checks, and developed X-rays: it was like watching images bloom on film like tiny secrets.

 ## The Day I Realized What I'd Been Given

One afternoon, a difficult teenage boy came in for an appointment. I was still a kid then, standing behind the front desk, watching without realizing I was being taught. Most adults tiptoe around that teenage attitude. My dad didn't. The kid was slouched in the chair, brushing off instructions, rolling his eyes like none of it mattered. My dad stopped mid-adjustment, leaned back slightly, and looked him straight in the eyes. "Hey," he said, calm but firm. "I'm here to help you. But I need you here with me." No lecture (those did happen on occasion), just a clear expectation.

He had this instinct for adjusting his approach to the person in front of him. Some kids needed steady quiet. Some needed loud truth. And because he was Italian, he could absolutely deliver a full-volume truth with hand gestures passed down through generations. He didn't just straighten teeth. He straightened paths. He gave kids the kind of perspective they pretended not to need but carried long after they left. It was mentorship from an unexpected place - an orthodontist's chair. That's the thing about leadership: **Leadership happens wherever people feel seen.**

And decades later, people still tell me:

"Your dad changed my life."

"Your father believed in my son when nobody else did."

"I didn't know what I was capable of until he told me."

This is the kind of leadership we rarely name - the kind that's learned through proximity, modeled through example.

The Blueprint Beneath My Feet 

Everything I've built grew out of those early years. Not in a straight line. Not intentionally. It happened because I was included in it long before I had words for what it was. I watched my parents offer what they had, even when it wasn't convenient. I watched potential be seen before it was obvious. Hard truths spoken with care. Consistency wasn't just discipline, it was a form of respect. Humanity mattered more than polish. At the time, it just felt like life. Looking back, I see it for what it was. Those moments became the ground I stood on. They shaped how I built businesses. How I taught in classrooms. How I led teams. They shaped how I show up in my community. And now, how I raise my son. Not because I copied a model, but because a pattern had already taken hold. Long before I had a title, a company, or a book, the foundation was already there-quietly doing its work.

It's the same foundation I'm offering to Dorian. And the same one available to you, no matter where you started. It's patterns. It's presence. It's the way leadership shows up in ordinary places: kitchens, offices, waiting rooms, where no one is watching closely, but everything is being learned.

Before I Had Words for It 

The lessons lived between appointment cards and angel tree sign-up sheets. Between orthodontist chairs and rink bleachers. Between quiet acts of service and adults who showed up without needing recognition. That office wasn't just a place where people got braces. It was a place where people were seen.

Once you grow up watching people be seen, you begin to understand something essential: Community isn't built by policies, programs, or perfect strategies. It's built when people decide to show up for one another. Again and again. In ordinary places. With no guarantee of anything in return. I've come to understand that leadership isn't something we wait to be granted. It's something we step into - in how we show up, how we serve, and how we invite others forward.

The D-Max Effect is what happens when that choice becomes intentional. When leadership moves beyond title or age and into daily action - at home, in work, and in community. It's what I carry forward now, into my work, my leadership, and the life I'm building with my son.

As Brendon Burchard writes in Millionaire Messenger, *"We have the opportunity to stand up, share our voice and expertise, and direct others to a greater future for themselves and for all of us. This is our time to lead and serve."*

This became the heartbeat of my life. And one day, many years later, it would become the heartbeat of a little boy who would stand at a hot cocoa table on a Saturday raising money so other kids could eat.

The Lineage of Service That Lives in My Son

People sometimes ask how Dorian went from a lemonade stand to organizing something as big as a Badge vs. Badge game - a charity softball game bringing police, firefighters, baseball, and an entire community together. The truth is, it started with a problem that he wanted to solve.

We worked together. We asked for help. We watched the momentum build as people felt included. That's how ideas expand-when exposure meets connection. I didn't know it at the time, but I learned the same way. Standing behind a front desk. Trusted with small responsibilities. Watching adults organize, collaborate, and follow through. What looks like a big idea is almost always a series of small ones connected over time. A stand. A table. A conversation. An invitation. That's how a community takes shape. It usually starts long before anyone realizes they're building something larger. It started here, with a little girl holding X-rays in a dim room, watching images appear slowly, not realizing she was learning how things come together-one small action at a time.

Chapter 2

THE HOUSE
THAT SERVICE BUILT

After my dad died, I went through boxes of paperwork - the kind every family keeps without really knowing why. Faded documents. Old programs. Stacks of papers that didn't look important until they suddenly were. That's when I found it. A small, stapled program from my elementary school. On the back was a page of ads-the kind local parents purchase to help cover printing costs. There, tucked between a florist and a pizza shop, was my dad's ad. No phone number. No address. Just his name and the words: *Proud supporter of our school.* Then I saw it again-his name listed as part of the development committee.

As a child, I had no idea how much time and energy he was quietly pouring into shaping not only my life, but entire classrooms of kids. Now, as a parent who understands what it takes to show up consistently: to organize, to follow through, to carry responsibility that often goes unseen, I see it differently. I recognize the hours. The coordination. The choice to say yes again and again. And I understand how much love lives inside that kind of effort. I sat on the floor holding that little program and felt the weight of a truth I had completely missed: My parents were building community long before I had language for it. They weren't explaining it. They weren't announcing it. They were modeling it through everyday choices that seemed small at the time but turned out to matter deeply. And that's when it became clear: We don't learn how to belong by being told. We learn by what we see modeled for us.

Building a Team Together

One such example was during my brother's time in high school. For years, no one stepped forward to build a hockey team. Then a small group of kids made it clear they wanted to play and a group of parents decided to make it happen. They didn't wait to be asked. They didn't wait to be appointed. They stepped forward together. These were parents who understood how systems get built. They knew how to organize, how to fundraise, how to divide responsibilities, and how to move together toward a shared goal. They didn't need a manual. They had each other. They built the program deliberately. First, they built a community. They made a team before there was ice time. They recruited enough kids to form a roster even those still learning to skate because teams are built by widening the circle, not narrowing it. Parents stepped into roles that matched their strengths. It was leadership in motion. And while the adults were building the team, I was absorbing all of it.

In the hockey world, I was what you'd call a rink rat. I grew up at the rink - eating concession stand food, sitting on cold bleachers, running around with other sisters whose lives revolved around practice schedules and game days. My brother played; we waited and watched. I watched adults collaborate. I watched people take responsibility. I watched a community form in real time. No one sat us down to explain leadership. They modeled it. That's what stays with me now. Modern leadership research talks about shared purpose, distributed responsibility, collective ownership, and relational trust. Those concepts weren't theories to me, they were lived experience. Hall-of-Fame coach Phil Jackson once said, *"The strength of the team is each individual member. The strength of each member is the team."* That was true on the ice. But it was even truer in the stands. Because teams don't form from talent alone. They form when people choose to lead together. That environment taught me one of the most enduring leadership lessons of my life: Great teams aren't joined. They're built collectively. One vision. Shared responsibility. Sustained commitment.

Lessons Etched in Childhood

Long before I understood leadership, I was surrounded by people practicing it. The parents and community members who shaped my childhood believed professionalism meant something simple: if you put your name on something, you showed up, followed through, and owned the outcome. Community meant that if something mattered, you didn't wait for someone else to fix it. You stepped in and helped build what was needed.

Professionalism - not the corporate kind, but the kind rooted in integrity - meant that if you put your name on something, you showed up, followed through, and owned the outcome.

Community meant that if something mattered, you didn't wait for someone else to fix it. You stepped in and helped build what was needed.

Responsibility meant understanding that your time, attention, and effort weren't just yours-they were meant to contribute to something larger.

Humility meant that real service didn't look for recognition. It focused on results.

These weren't lessons taught in a classroom. They were learned by being included in real work, around real people, with real stakes.

 ## Understanding the Gaps

I share these stories not because they're universal, but because they shaped how I learned to lead. You may not have grown up surrounded by adults who modeled shared responsibility, integrity, or community-building. You may not have had a clear example to follow. And that matters because leadership isn't built by pretending we all start in the same place. **Leadership doesn't require a perfect past.** It requires a willingness to participate in the present. You don't need to recreate what you didn't have. You can build what's missing-intentionally, imperfectly, and over time.

 ## Legacy in Plain Sight

One afternoon, while packing up after the holidays, I pulled out the box to store our nativity set. Tucked inside was a letter my dad had written to me in 2006.

I read it every year-a quiet ritual. But this time, sitting on the floor surrounded by ornaments and tissue paper, something shifted. Not because the words were new, but because I could suddenly see how far they had traveled. Not just into my life, but through it. What I'd absorbed as a child. What I'd practiced as an adult. What I was now building alongside my son.

Reading his words, I could picture us at the dining room table-the steady rhythm of his voice, the way he leaned in when something mattered. For a moment, it felt like he was talking to me again, not from the past, but right there, reminding me of who he trusted me to become.

That's when I understood: leadership doesn't announce itself while it's working. It moves forward quietly, through example, repetition, and care. His letter starts with noticing something was missing: Joseph's staff. It was the last set available, so instead of returning it, he found a small stick-nearly perfect in shape-and made one himself. In his letter, he explained why. *"It was at St. Joseph's, I learned how to be a dad."*

When my father was a student at St. Michael's College, he worked at St. Joseph's Child Center-an orphanage home to children from infancy through eighth grade, run by the Sisters of Providence. What began as a college job quickly became something more.

The orphanage was enormous-two wings, one for boys and one for girls, with the nuns living in between. There was a school, a gym with a movie screen, a library, separate dining rooms, and acres of land. They were trying to build a home.

They organized sports. Took the kids swimming, hiking, and to the movies. They even had a school bus. My dad ran a tutoring program that paired college students one-on-one with children who were struggling. *"It worked,"* he wrote. *"And I learned that no child is dull - only uncertain."* Before a child could learn, he realized, they had to feel peace inside.

As he watched children blossom-confidence growing alongside reading and comprehension, he learned patience and humor. He was only a college student, but he was learning how to raise a family. And more than that, he learned that helping a child grow was one of the most important tasks a person could undertake. *"A blessing beyond belief. There were no awards. No trophies. None were needed."*

Because holding a child, helping unlock their heart, and watching them soar-knowing the change would last a lifetime-was priceless.

Then he returned to Joseph. He said, *"Joseph doesn't stand in the front. He doesn't have many speaking lines in Christmas plays. But he's there. Really there. A stepfather. A steady presence. A man who understood that every child is a gift."* The letter ended with a reflection on the missing staff. *"In a way, it was never missing. He had lent it to me years ago."* Reading his words again, I could see it clearly: leadership that doesn't announce itself. Lessons passed through presence, not performance. This wasn't about being exceptional. It was about showing up again and again. And consistency is what builds trust long before anyone calls it leadership. And once you see leadership that way, you start to notice it everywhere. In the people who quietly take responsibility. In the ones who stay when it would be easier to leave. In the moments that don't look important at the time but turn out to be pivotal in life. Long before anyone realizes they're leading. But knowing what leadership looks like doesn't guarantee you'll be able to rebuild it the same way.

Chapter 3

BREAKING CYCLES, REWRITING FUTURES

There are moments in adulthood that divide life into a before and an after. Mine came with divorce.

Dorian was just two - still learning words, routines, and what "home" meant when I realized I wasn't going to be able to give him the same upbringing I had. Not in the way it looked. Not in the structure. Not in the simplicity or security of two parents, one home, one steady rhythm. And even though no one prepares you for this part, the grief is real and deep. There is a unique ache in realizing you can't recreate the home that shaped you and that what's being asked of you now is to imagine something new. Not because you failed, but because life changed and required a different kind of courage. Alongside that grief was a truth I couldn't ignore: I still had a future to shape. For myself. For Dorian.

That realization didn't arrive with confidence or clarity. It arrived slowly, in small moments when I gave myself permission to imagine differently. Not a smaller life. Not a compromised one. But a future wide enough to hold who we could become. A version of family defined not by structure, but by intention. Not by perfection, but by presence. Not by what was lost, but by what could still be created. I stopped measuring our future against the past. And started authoring one that fit us fully. That choice changed everything. Because when you stop trying to replicate what no longer exists, you create space for something more honest, more flexible, and more alive than what you first envisioned. And that work - the work of imagining an abundant future, even when you feel unfinished is the most powerful modeling a child will ever witness.

Entrepreneurial Thinking When the Blueprint Collapses

My identity changed overnight. Wife to single mother. Partner to sole point of stability. What remained was my instinct to build when there was no clear path forward.

I had learned early that if the path didn't exist, you make one. I had watched my parents do it years before - creating a hockey program from nothing more than belief, effort, and a willingness to figure things out as they went.

When I opened my coworking space, I didn't know how to build walls. So I learned. My business partner taught me how to use a table saw and frame a wall so we could stretch every dollar. My mom helped paint. Friends showed up after work and on weekends to assemble furniture, lifting things that were heavier than expected, laughing through exhaustion.

It wasn't about doing everything myself. It was about letting others be part of the work. About asking for help without apology. About showing what responsibility looks like when you don't have all the answers.

I wasn't just building a business-I was building a living example of what possibility looks like when community is part of the equation. And Dorian was watching. He didn't see perfection or polish. He saw effort. He saw problems met with curiosity instead of fear. He saw setbacks treated as clues - data points to decode faster next time.

He's learning that same instinct now, hunched over a Rubik's cube, studying every scrambled pattern his friends - kids who compete and solve in thirteen seconds flat - have handed him. Every failed solve isn't a dead end. It's a faster route waiting to be found.

The Relationship That Held Me Together

Before that season of rebuilding, there was Eliza.

We met in college. We did life together. She helped me start my first business. She listened to ideas and helped me map them out. She understood the pressure of being both a mother and a business owner because she was living it too. She was my confidant. My sounding board. My steady place to land. The person who could hold both my ambition and my exhaustion without judgment. She was my best friend.

When I was in uncharted territory- newly navigating single motherhood, entrepreneurship, and reinvention - she became both my anchor and my sail. She steadied me when I felt unmoored and pushed me forward when I doubted my direction. We shared the same dual pull: wanting to give our children everything, while also feeling called to serve our communities and build meaningful work. We understood the impossible tension of holding the desire to be both fully present at home and fully impactful in the world.

We talked often about the myth of "having it all," and how real life rarely matches that phrase-not perfectly, not without cost, not without trade-offs. But we also talked about the beauty of having *enough*: purpose, presence, and people.

And then she got sick. Her illness rearranged the air around us. Conversations shifted from plans to priorities. Time became sharper, more precious. The future felt less like a guarantee and more like a gift. When she later passed, everything in my world reordered.

There are losses that create new layers of identity, and hers was one of them. I understood instantly-viscerally-that my time with Dorian, no matter how long it will be and no matter how close we are, is **limited**. One day he will grow up, leave home, and build his own life. One day he will lead his own mission. One day I will have a different role-not the center, but the witness. My job isn't to shape every moment-it's to help him become who he's meant to be…and then, little by little, learn to step back with love and pride so he can become it.

When You Weren't Shown How - Learning to Solve Problems Together

Dorian and I started volunteering during COVID. Like so many families, our world suddenly felt small. Isolated. Quiet in a way that didn't feel peaceful-just lonely. I wanted to show him that even when everything shuts down, connection is still possible. That impact doesn't disappear just because circumstances change. And honestly? We loved it. Volunteering gave us something steady when so much felt uncertain. Dorian made friends. He felt useful. Seen. Part of something bigger than himself. That year, he was honored as Volunteer of the Year by Heart of Maine United Way. Because it was COVID, the ceremony happened over Zoom. Faces appeared in little boxes. Kind words were shared. Certificates were held up to webcams. It was an incredible event, but when the call ended, Dorian was quiet. He was disappointed that he hadn't won the gift certificate to a local bike shop that was given away during the ceremony. I was puzzled. He had just received a major community award, and he had several bikes sitting outside our house. Why was that the thing he was focused on? Then he said something that stopped me cold. *"I wanted to give it to kids who don't have bikes,"* he explained. *"I love riding so much. I want other kids to be able to do that too."*

At that moment, I realized he wasn't disappointed for himself. He was disappointed for someone else. What I had missed, because I was too quick to interpret the moment through my own adult lens, was that he already understood what the award meant. To him, it wasn't just recognition. **It was confirmation**. Proof that he could make other people's lives better. He experienced it as an invitation to keep going, to do more, to widen the circle. The gift certificate wasn't about wanting another bike. It was about wanting to give bikes to kids who didn't have one. I felt the quiet sting of realizing how quickly I had misread him. How easily I had projected my own assumptions onto a child who was already thinking beyond himself. In that moment, the lesson wasn't his alone-it was mine.

So I took a breath and did what parenting so often requires in real time: I modeled problem-solving. *We don't need a gift certificate to get kids bikes!"* I told him. So we decided to do a fundraiser. I was thinking we could raise money for four or five bikes. We built a budget for bikes and helmets but decided that we should reach out to the Boys & Girls Club to confirm a modest need. What we learned instead was that the need for bikes was far bigger than the goal we had set. The scope grew fast, and I knew that this was going to take more than a few lemonade stands.

We worked hard. We shared the story. Momentum came in waves-a burst of generosity here, a quiet stretch there. And then came the part that always shows up in fundraising: the lull. The point where the messages slow down. The donations stop coming in as easily. The goal still feels far away. There was a moment when I had to say out loud, *We might not meet our goal."* And when things felt hardest, it wasn't ambition that kept us going. It was the thought of a kid not having a bike - of a child missing out on something as simple and joyful as riding alongside their friends. That was enough to keep going. We adjusted. We asked again. We stayed visible even when it felt uncomfortable. Then, as often happens in this work, another organization stepped in to help close the gap.

In the end, Dorian got to deliver brand - new bikes and helmets to kids at a Boys & Girls Club of Bangor. They organized a bike rodeo around the giving away of the bikes. Dorian even brought his bike to ride through a fun obstacle course alongside kids who were riding their new bikes for the very first time. I saw the shift I hadn't fully understood months earlier - the lingering disappointment after the ceremony, the fixation on a bike shop gift card. It had never been about winning something. It was about building something and being there when it came to life. That was the moment his happiness replaced the disappointment.

The D-Max Effect lives in moments like this. When we don't rush to explain away a child's disappointment, but pause long enough to listen. When we treat frustration as information instead of attitude. And when we invite kids into the work of solving the problems they notice, they don't just feel better - they grow into people who believe they can make things better. That belief is what lasts.

Chapter 4

TACO TUESDAY

If you've read the *Power of Transparency*, you already know that the story of Dorian's early life didn't begin quietly. It began on a **Taco Tuesday** with community, chaos, kindness, and a restaurant full of people who became extensions of our family. That book holds the stories of Dorian's first years - the season when everything felt unpredictable, when life was being rebuilt in real time. It was the period surrounding my divorce, when nothing looked the way I had planned, and yet somehow everything worked because people showed up for us in ways I didn't fully comprehend at the time and I still don't know how to thank them deeply enough.

Messy Life, Open Arms

Running a restaurant with a baby meant there was almost no separation between business and motherhood. A high chair lived next to the prep station. Toys rolled under the counter.

More than once, a customer who came in for burritos ended up holding my baby so I could finish their order. And here's the truth: no one ever made me feel like I had to choose. They just stepped in. According to the Kauffman Foundation, 42% of new businesses in America are now started by women, and nearly 61% of those founders are also mothers. And when you ask them why they do it, most give the same answer: *"Because I want my children to see what's possible."*

Customers passing Dorian from one set of arms to another were doing exactly that - raising me up, raising him up, raising the community up. Walking into that restaurant as a mother wasn't a liability; it was a signal: **This is what it looks like when women refuse to choose between their dreams and their children. This is what it looks like to have both!** That was my reality. Running the cash register, holding Dorian on my hip. Answering a customer's question while picking Cheerios off the prep table. Handling payroll after bedtime, writing marketing plans with a baby monitor buzzing beside me. And because he grew up witnessing it, community wasn't something Dorian learned later-it was the air he breathed. He saw people step in. He saw service without fanfare. He saw adults make room for a baby in their day like it was the most natural thing in the world. That little restaurant, with a toddler eating in a dining room full of people, was his first classroom in leadership, community, and generosity.

The Fire and the Parade

Then came the fire that tore through downtown Gardiner -

one of those moments when a whole community holds its breath at once. Firefighters from multiple towns rushed in. Streets were filled with smoke, exhaustion, and the sound of people trying to save what mattered. My instinct was immediate: Empty the coolers. Bring what we have. Help where we can. We hauled out cases of drinks and whatever food made sense to feed the firefighters and those who lost their buildings and livelihood.

A few days later, an annual parade took place. Downtown was still hurting. Buildings had been destroyed by the fire. The loss felt heavy and unresolved-the kind that lingers in the air long after the smoke clears. Our community was tired, shaken, and still taking stock of what had been lost. And yet, we gathered anyway.

We walked in the parade, thanking everyone who had come to our aid. Dorian was just a toddler then. While the adults walked with purpose and gratitude, he ran ahead, weaving in and out, handing out stickers, offering high-fives, shaking hands. He didn't understand the scale of the loss or the logistics of recovery. What he understood was presence. He was right in the middle of it. Not shielded from the moment. Not set apart from the work of community. Just included.

And in that simple inclusion, something lasting was forming - the belief that when things fall apart, you show up; that gratitude is something you do with your whole body; that even small hands have a place in moments that matter. That wasn't a lesson we sat down to teach. It was something he absorbed by being there.

 Early Signs and What They Truly Mean

People often look for a single moment that explains leadership. A spark. A trait. A reason someone "turned out the way they did." That's not how this story begins. Dorian's leadership didn't emerge from recognition or praise. It didn't come from being told he was special or exceptional. It came from something far more ordinary and far more powerful. From the beginning, he was included. He sat at tables where real work was happening. He listened as adults worked through problems, showed up for one another, and followed through - not perfectly, but consistently. No one framed this as a lesson. No one called it leadership training. It was simply his environment. In that environment, belonging wasn't passive. Being there came with responsibility. Participation was expected. Contribution was welcomed. Helping wasn't presented as a virtue-it was just normal. Community wasn't something people talked about. It was something they practiced. That's the part that matters most. It's about what surrounded him while he was becoming. Because children don't form their sense of purpose through big speeches or defining moments. They absorb it through repetition-through the small interactions that happen over and over again.

Being invited to help. Being trusted with something real. Being included in work that matters. Those moments don't feel significant while they're happening. They feel ordinary. But they're not. They are wiring beliefs about who you are and where you belong.

Long before a child can articulate confidence, they learn whether they are capable. Long before they understand service, they learn whether their presence matters. Long before they chase purpose, they learn whether contribution is expected of them or reserved for someone else.

That's the D-Max Effect. It isn't about raising exceptional kids. It's about raising kids who believe they are part of something and therefore responsible for it. The restaurant. The meetings. The fundraisers. The fire across the street. None of these were designed as lessons. They were ordinary moments lived openly. They were invitations. And he accepted them. Every family has moments like this - messy, real, unplanned - waiting to become part of a child's blueprint for how to show up in the world. Ours just happened to start on Taco Tuesday.

Chapter 5

The Moment His Heart
Became Visible to Others

There are moments in parenting when something inside you shifts, not because of anything dramatic, but because a small act reveals something undeniable about who your child is becoming. For me, that realization came in a soup kitchen on Thanksgiving, surrounded by the smell of warm food and the sound of my dad playing the piano-the way only he could, with a kind of generosity that lifted people from the inside out.

A Little Boy and a Cart Full of Pie

Dorian was maybe four or five years old then. We put him on pie duty! The cart was taller than him, and he leaned his entire body forward to push it, inch by inch, serving the people at their tables.

Most kids that age want to be served first. They want the biggest slice. They want to sit and enjoy the celebration. And to be honest, he wanted pie too. He knew that in that room, wanting wasn't the same as needing. He recognized at a very young age that he was there to help serve, not to be served. It reminded me of something Simon Sinek wrote in Leaders Eat Last: *"Leadership is not about being in charge. It's about taking care of those in your charge."* Dorian was taking care of his neighbors-quietly, instinctively, generously.

It Wasn't Politeness - It Was Character

There are "good kids"- the ones who follow instructions and mind their manners. And then there are children whose goodness isn't compliance, but identity. Children who see needs. Children who step in. Children whose hearts move before their minds do. Dorian wasn't trying to impress anyone. He simply believed helping was the right thing to do. That pie cart moment stayed with me for years. But it wasn't the last time it appeared.

Friday Night Lights and DJ Sparkles: The "Ask Anyway" Moment

Years later, that same instinct resurfaced, this time in the middle of a loud, energetic Friday night free skate at the ice arena. I wasn't there. But Dorian told me the story afterward in the kind of breathless excitement that tells you something small meant something big. The rink's DJ, "DJ Sparkles" is one of his favorite people. She hands out bracelets, lifts up every kid who comes her way, and knows how to turn a cold arena into the warmest place in town. She had announced clearly that she was done taking song requests for the night. The kids heard her. The rule was set. But Dorian went up anyway. Not asking for a trendy song. He asked her to play a Christmas song - something warm and nostalgic, something that would soften the edges of the night and make the rink feel like a shared moment instead of a scattered one.

He told me she looked at him with a sparkle in her eyes - the kind adults get when a child's sincerity stirs something in them and she simply said: *"Why not?"* She played it. He said the energy shifted, to become connected. So he asked *again*. This time "DJ Sparkles" didn't just play the song. She leaned into the microphone and said: *"This one's from D-Max!"* It wasn't the announcement that mattered. It was the lesson: **Ask anyway. Kindness makes room for exceptions.** Hope is worth the risk. Dorian didn't change the whole arena, he changed the moment. And that's what leaders do.

The Quiet Unfolding of Who He Was Becoming 

These weren't grand gestures or spotlight moments, and they weren't planned. They were small acts - a pie cart, song requests, gentle risks- revealing a child whose instinct was to make things better, even in the smallest ways. Those instincts weren't a phase or a good week, and they certainly weren't accidental. They are his character. They are his wiring. This is who he is.

I began to see him differently - not just as a little kid, but as a leader in the most human sense of the word. A leader who believes in asking anyway, who looks for the one thing that could make a moment warmer and chooses it, whose first instinct is simply to care.

"Through his book and visit, Dorian modeled leadership in action: he showed that one person's voice, even before adulthood, can encourage others to act kindly, help others, and make an enormous positive impact. Dorian's calm presence and compassionate spirit inspired meaningful conversations about empathy, responsibility, and kindness.

Through his visit, he showed our students that one person's voice - even before adulthood - can encourage others to act with care and make a real difference. Many left saying they wanted to 'be like D-Max.'"

- 2nd Grade Teacher

Chapter 6

Raising A Heart-Led Leader While Rebuilding Yourself

No one really prepares you for how jarring the shift can be. One day, you're living inside a shared rhythm - two adults, a routine, a sense of "we." And then suddenly, you're not. You're learning how to be a mother in a completely new way, while grieving the life you thought you were building.

There's a version of motherhood we're often shown - quiet mornings, predictable routines, milestones neatly recorded and celebrated on a calendar. And then there's the kind that unfolds when the ground is still moving beneath you. When you're piecing together a new identity, figuring out finances, rebuilding confidence, and redefining stability-while guiding a child who is also trying to understand who they are in the middle of it all. That kind of motherhood isn't polished. It's brave. It's tender. And it's deeply human. Those years after my divorce didn't feel like chapters in a story. They felt like survival strung together with hope. But what I didn't know then, and what only hindsight reveals, is that those years were also the foundation of something else: Dorian was learning how to become a heart-led leader, and I was learning how to become one too.

Mothering Through Transition

When your life is in transition, you parent differently. You love differently. You lead differently. You're honest without having to explain everything. You're strong without pretending to be unbreakable. You're present even when the future feels blurry.

Some days I felt like I was giving him the best of me. Some days I felt like I was giving him whatever pieces life left over with a side of McDonald's for dinner.

But what he saw wasn't instability-it was a mother who kept trying. He saw me build businesses, rebuild confidence, and rearrange our lives until the pieces began to fit again. He saw decisions made with integrity, even when they were difficult. He saw a life that wasn't perfect, but was purposeful. And purpose, it turns out, is one of the best teachers a child can have.

Teaching Leadership Without a Textbook (But With a Framework)

When I began teaching at the college level, I didn't rely on traditional textbooks. Not because I dismissed theory, but because my life had never unfolded according to one. Instead, I gave my students books that reflected how business and management actually show up in the real world-how organizations grow, how people behave, and how decisions ripple outward.

Give and Take - by Adam Grant
The E-Myth - by Michael Gerber
Who Moved My Cheese? - by Spencer Johnson

They were operating systems for understanding work, value, and change. Books that put language to what they were already witnessing. Adam Grant writes, *"The most meaningful way to succeed is to help others succeed."* That idea didn't stay on a page. My students watched it play out in real time. Every semester, they were given an assignment most business classes never ask of students: Design and execute a real fundraiser for a real non-profit. Not hypothetically. Not on paper. Not "someday." Now!

They weren't just assigned a project. They were introduced to a nonprofit in our community. I would invite someone from the organization to come into the classroom and stand in front of the students- not as a guest speaker, but as a partner. They shared their mission. The problem they were trying to solve. The people or cause they serve. And suddenly this wasn't theoretical anymore.

The students asked questions and some shared their own stories. They talked about nonprofits that had helped their families. Food pantries. Community programs. Organizations that had quietly stepped in during hard seasons. For a few of them, the nonprofit standing in front of the room wasn't just an organization, it was something they had personally experienced.

This wasn't just about learning how nonprofits work. It was about recognizing the role they play in real lives including their own. Instead of simply benefiting from that work, the students were being invited into it. They weren't just hearing about service. They were being shown a path to give back to something that had once given to them.

What do you need most right now?
What's the hardest part of the work?
How could we help?

From that moment on, the nonprofit wasn't just a case study. They became collaborators. Throughout the semester, the partnership continued. The nonprofit checked in with the class. They answered questions. They shared updates from the field. They helped guide the students as ideas turned into plans and plans turned into action. It wasn't a simulation. It was a real collaboration- students and community partners working side by side, learning from each other, and building something meaningful together.

In groups they built a plan, created and executed a marketing strategy, hosted an event, and reported on the impact. The stakes were real. So were the people they served. In the final class, I invited our nonprofit partner back to hear from the students about the impact they made and also to receive thousands of dollars raised. In that moment, the pride was unmistakable. They had done something real. You could see it in their smiles and the confidence in their voices as they shared what they had done. They were proud of themselves and excited to talk about the impact they had made.

One student reflected: *"My first reaction was, 'How am I*

*supposed to do this? I'm too young. I don't have enough experience.'
I felt doubt before I even started. But then we watched the video
of Dorian delivering food to the community. He was six years
younger than me and still figuring things out-but he was doing it
anyway. It mattered. If he could learn while helping others, then
I could try too."*

But the most important part of that moment wasn't the video. It was what it unlocked in her. Seeing someone younger simply take action changed the question in her mind from *"Am I capable of this?"* to *"Why not try?"* She stopped waiting for permission and began building a project of her own, raising both funds and awareness for a nonprofit she cared about.

That's the D-Max Effect: leadership learned through **action, proximity, and permission,** long before confidence or credentials arrive.

Letting Them See the Whole Picture

My life became a real-time case study in how people navigate hard seasons and keep moving anyway. There was a semester I taught when my dad was put on hospice. I had a feeling that the time was close so I moved class online because I couldn't leave him. I told my students the truth-that sometimes the most important decision you make isn't the most productive one, but the most human one.

He passed away that night.

Spring break followed, giving me space to grieve. When we returned, I opened the first class back differently than I ever had before. I created a PowerPoint. (I never use PowerPoint.)

The first slide asked a simple question:

What will they say at your funeral?

Then I showed them photos. I told them stories. A legacy built through service, consistency, and showing up for others. I realized I wasn't just sharing someone else's story - I was revealing the why that was shaping my own life. My students weren't just learning how to manage time or organize projects. They were learning something deeper: how to decide what truly matters when the moment arrives. Along the way, they received something I never wrote into the syllabus- bonus life lessons that extend far beyond a single semester.

That wasn't the only moment when life rewrote the lesson plan. Eliza was diagnosed with stage four cancer. By the time the doctors found it, it had already spread throughout her body. She was a mother of four beautiful children. The kind of person whose presence anchored a room.

She called me and said she needed help. She believed she was going to prove the doctors wrong. But if they were right, we were looking at months - not years.

Suddenly the fight was immediate and unrelenting. Again, I brought the moment into my classroom. Eliza needed help in the same way the nonprofits my students were working with needed help.

So we did what we knew how to do. We built something.

Planning the fundraisers felt like the business brainstorming sessions we had shared for years - the energy, the ideas, the back and forth. Except now the stakes were different. Even on her hardest days, Eliza would show up to those conversations with fire. She had opinions. She had vision. She was still herself. And in those moments, the work wasn't just about raising money. It was about giving her something to look forward to and the resources to fight. A way to see - visibly, undeniably - how many people loved her and were standing in this battle beside her.

That's one of the most powerful things a community can do for someone who is suffering: make their love visible. Not just felt. Visible.

We weren't just raising money. We were racing against time for someone we loved — making sure that whatever happened, she would know we had shown up completely. That we had tried everything. That she was never, not for a single moment, alone in this fight.

While my students were building campaigns for their partner nonprofits, I was running one of my own. I shared the numbers with them. The outreach. The strategy. The moments that worked and the ones that didn't.

I wasn't just teaching leadership. I was modeling it in real time.

At the end of the semester, students reflected on what they had learned. One reflection stopped me in my tracks. A student wrote:

"People cared more than I thought they would. This surprised me because I assumed everyone would just glance at my posts and move on. But people actually read them. They absorbed them. I realized I wasn't just asking for donations - I was helping people see how they could make a difference."

While they were learning these lessons in the classroom,

I was learning them alongside them. I wasn't standing at the front teaching a case study. I was in it with them.

For another student, the lesson showed up in a different way. Unlike the previous semester, this course was offered asynchronously. Students weren't working together with a single nonprofit partner in the classroom. Instead, they were asked to identify a nonprofit that mattered personally to them. They would reach out, interview the organization, and then design a full fundraising campaign on their own. Each student built their own project from the ground up. One student chose her daughter's Montessori school. She was a nontraditional student balancing work, family, and school- fitting coursework into the margins of a busy life. Because the school was already woven into her daily life, the project became something more than coursework. It became a chance to strengthen relationships and step into leadership in a place where she was already showing up. The following semester, I received an email from her. She wanted me to know that because of the project, she had been asked to join the board of the Montessori school she had spent the semester supporting. What began as a grade in a class had changed the trajectory of her relationship with the school all because she showed up, took responsibility, and used her voice to strengthen a community she was already part of.

Chapter 7

The First Fundraiser:
The Spark That Lit Everything

Before the awards. Before the media stories. Before state-wide partnerships or large scale fundraisers. Before any of that, there was a boy who noticed that some kids didn't have snacks.

At age seven, Dorian partnered with a local boutique candle maker. The idea started in my coworking space I had opened. One of the members had a small side business making the best smelling candles. When Dorian began thinking about ways to raise money to help other kids, I suggested he talk with her and see if collaboration might be possible. So he did. She listened to him. Really listened. She took his idea seriously and said yes to exploring what they could create together. That simple moment - an adult choosing to believe in a kid's idea - is something I've come to recognize as a quiet engine behind the D-Max Effect. Curiosity met creativity. Generosity met possibility. The owner created a custom candle with a bright mandarin - citrus scent and a name that felt exactly like him: **D-Max Power Juice.**

Thirty percent of every candle sold would go toward buying

snacks for children in need within a ten-mile radius of our home. There were no committees. No complicated systems. No long-term vision decks. Just a kid with an idea. An adult who listened. And a simple goal: Make sure no kids go hungry.

By the end of the fundraiser, he had raised just over five hundred dollars. Modest by any large scale measure, but enormous in what it represented.

A local news station reached out to do an interview. And for the first time, he was seen. Really seen. Not by family who loved him, not by neighbors who knew him - but by a world that had no reason to pay attention, and chose to anyway. There he was on television, a kid with a big heart who had decided a community problem was his to help solve, sharing his message in his own words. The feeling of *I am seen. I am heard.* - that kind of validation doesn't come with an age requirement. It just lands. And it landed for him.

Every kid processes the world by making something - a drawing, a fort, a story whispered into a stuffed animal's ear. Dorian just happened to do it on camera, with a cause, and with that particular brand of heart that makes strangers stop scrolling.

After the fundraiser wrapped up, we headed to the store with cash in our pockets. Dorian practically bounced down the aisles. We stood there doing the math together- counting bills, checking prices, figuring out how far the money could stretch. Every choice mattered. Every dollar meant more snacks for kids. He moved through the aisle with the kind of focus only a kid on a mission has. "No one wants the plain ones," he told me, scanning the shelves. "These run out first." "And kids love these." He wasn't guessing. He knew. We filled the cart talking about what kids love to eat at school, and what would make someone feel excited to open their backpack instead of singled out. It wasn't just shopping. It was a seven-year-old making sure other kids had something good waiting for them.

He wasn't watching me make choices for him. He was making them. That sense of ownership mattered. The snacks weren't abstract anymore. They were his responsibility - his follow-through on a promise he had made.

I did offer suggestions. Regularly. Enthusiastically. Every single one was vetoed with the same patient, slightly pitying look and a variation of *Mom, no one actually likes those.*

We packed the car and prepared to deliver them to the school but the plan got accelerated because COVID arrived quickly. Schools closed. Routines vanished. We rushed to deliver the snacks before the doors locked, unsure what the coming days would bring.

We only knew this: Children who relied on school meals would now be home and hungry. As we drove home after dropping off snacks, a school bus ahead of us slowed - not to pick up students, but to drop off bags of food. Children and parents waited at the ends of their long driveways. One stop after another. Mile after mile The need was more than I had imagined. It's easy to read statistics and think you understand the need. But seeing it was different. Watching those bags handed out along quiet country roads, seeing the families waiting - we could see the faces behind the need.

I spoke as we drove, giving words to what he was noticing - not a lecture, just a widening of the frame. I tried to hold back tears, the kind that come when pride and heartbreak arrive at the same time. He was seeing the world more clearly, and I was seeing it too, through the eyes of a parent whose heart ached at what children begin to carry long before they fully understand it.

That's the lesson. Not the kind you explain - the kind you *feel.* Your children are ready for it too, if you're willing to take them there.

I was reminded of a quote by John Gardner, one I've returned to many times, that captured exactly what was unfolding: *"Meaning is not something you stumble across. Meaning is something you build."*

On that rural road, Dorian began assembling the earliest pieces of his own meaning, drawn from what he was witnessing, what he felt, and what he believed mattered. That candle fundraiser was not the culmination of anything. It was the ignition. The moment intention met action. The moment action met impact.

This is what I want every reader to understand: Leadership doesn't begin with grand plans. Change doesn't start with sweeping gestures. It begins when someone notices a need and chooses not to look away. A citrus-scented candle. A rural bus route. A handful of snacks. A realization that I can help. This is how leadership begins. This is how impact takes root. This is how meaning is built - long before anyone knows your name.

Chapter 8

Why Consistency Is More Powerful Than Talent

The Maine Venture Fund hosts an annual competition called the Maine Startup Challenge - a statewide opportunity for students and entrepreneurs to take an idea, turn it into a one-page business plan, and compete for cash prizes.

When I first suggested Dorian enter, it wasn't about winning, though that would have been an incredible honor. It felt like a meaningful homeschool lesson. We sat at the table together and worked through a business model canvas, talking about customers, costs, value, and impact. He had been doing this kind of work for so long that he moved through the model with quickness and confidence.

Fast forward a few months, and there he was standing on a stage, accepting $1,000 in prize money after winning the K-8 age group. He was overcome with excitement, his first reaction pure and immediate: *"Wow. I just made a thousand dollars."*

And that's when the lesson shifted. This wasn't merch profit he'd watched slowly add up. This was different. This money came with a tax form. Plus opportunity to see how money really works. Revenue isn't the same as income, taxes are part of building something real, and that the way you handle money can either create momentum or limit what's possible.

This wasn't entirely new territory for him. He already understood profit and loss. When he sold merchandise, he built a plan that factored in costs, revenue, and sales tax. What we were doing now was simply expanding the lesson- taking concepts he already knew and applying them in a bigger, more meaningful way. When we raised money for fundraisers, the dollars moved quickly and clearly from people who wanted to help straight to the nonprofit that needed it. But this was different. Now there were more decisions attached to every dollar.

Winning didn't come with milestones to meet or reports to submit. There were no expectations about what the money should become. But instead of leaving it there, I expanded on the framework he already understood- talking through bigger milestones, more thoughtful planning, and the responsibility that comes with managing more money. This prize money could easily disappear on the fun things every kid wants or become a foundation for something bigger. How we treated it would shape not just the next project, but the habits he was building around leadership, trust, and decision-making.

This small amount of capital gave us permission to think differently - to think bigger. The question shifted from *Is this enough?* to *How much impact can we build?*

He wasn't thinking like a kid with money. He was thinking like a leader learning what responsibility actually feels like. Being the competitive kid that he is, he was excited to put that money to work and watch it grow. And in that moment, I realized something important: he wasn't just learning about money. He was learning about possibility. Every decision was a chance to ask a bigger question: What could this become?

Watching Him Build Something He'd Never Seen Befo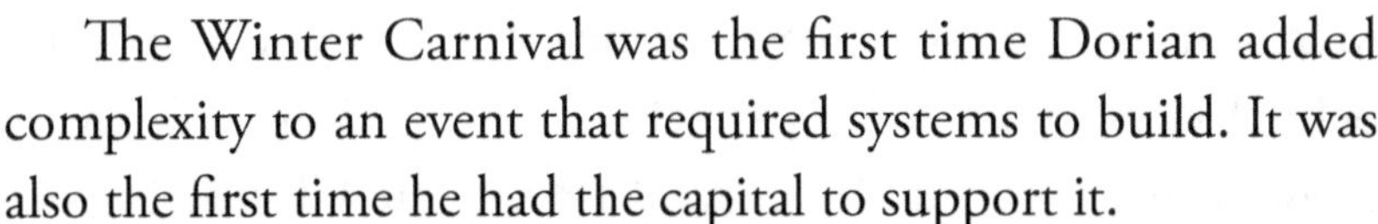

The Winter Carnival was the first time Dorian added complexity to an event that required systems to build. It was also the first time he had the capital to support it.

Winning the Maine Venture Fund competition gave him the cash to rent the rec center and throw a truly fun, community-wide event. But with that opportunity came a leveling up. He had to explain the vision clearly enough that adults would say yes. He had to invite others to join him because unlike a lemonade stand, this event had a lot of moving pieces and required lots of helping hands. He raised sponsorships not because he needed the money to get started, but because he wanted others to be part of it.

Winning the $1,000 prize had given him something important- confidence. An organization had believed in his idea. They had invested in him. That belief made the whole thing feel possible. But he didn't want to build the event alone. He wanted the party to belong to the community. Sponsorships became his way of inviting others in- local businesses, neighbors, and supporters who could help make the day more fun, more generous, and more memorable for the kids who would be there.

He understood something intuitively that many adults miss: inviting others in isn't a sign of scarcity - it's a sign of leadership.

Businesses wanted to be part of something positive. Community groups wanted a reason to show up. Sponsors weren't just funding an event - they were joining a moment that mattered. He asked because he wanted people to feel ownership, pride, and connection. He didn't want "good enough." He wanted it to be extra fun. So we asked for help and people responded.

Chi Omega, a sorority at the University of Maine, stepped in to serve hot cocoa and manage stations. The Brewer Community School PTA took on face painting and outreach. Volunteers showed up-more than twenty of them. The City of Brewer shared his flyer through their community newsletter, extending the invitation far beyond our immediate circle. Watching it all come together, I realized this wasn't just an event- it was a shift.

# The Moment I Knew This Was Bigger Than an Event

As families filtered out of the Brewer Rec that afternoon, I felt the familiar mix of relief and exhaustion that comes after pulling off something big. We got into the car and started the drive home. That's when I saw her. A mother walking through the cold with four kids-the same kids I had just watched run, laugh, and spill hot cocoa on themselves moments before.

No car. Just a mom doing everything she could to provide for her kids in the way she knew how. They were bundled up against the bitter cold, one child in her arms, the others pressing close, their laughter already fading into the quiet of a Maine winter afternoon.

And in that moment, the entire day reoriented itself. The fact that they had to walk home in that cold, with no car to shield them, was humbling.

The weekend before, we had been in Canada for hockey: hotel rooms, knee hockey in the halls, adventures that filled our calendar without much thought. Our weekends are often full. For this family, this was the weekend. A free event, within walking distance of home. As we drove past them, the weight of it settled in. We talked honestly about the privilege we carry. About how different our weekends look. About how grateful we are to be in a position where we can make someone else's weekend lighter, warmer, more joyful.

He stared out the window for a long moment before saying, *"I'm really glad they came."*

Leadership isn't about doing it all. It's about seeing who's carrying more than their share and choosing, again and again, to help carry it. If these kids needed snacks at school, we knew they would be there.

The Pattern I Couldn't Ignore Anymore 

I saw it not just in the Winter Carnival, but in every fund-raiser, every classroom visit, every moment he chose to act instead of looking away. Over time, a pattern began to emerge - one I had watched repeat itself across years, settings, and ages.

It wasn't a strategy. It wasn't a parenting hack. It was a rhythm.

And once I saw it clearly, I realized something that wouldn't let me go: this wasn't unique to us. It is teachable, repeatable, and available to anyone willing to look at leadership differently.

That realization became the reason this book exists.

The D-Max Effect is built on a simple truth: children don't need to be taught leadership - they need to be included in it.

Over time, I began to see five repeatable patterns show up again and again:

Invite early - Let children and others into real work before they feel ready.

Model visibly - Choose effort over polish. Process over perfection. Courage over comfort.

Practice kindness daily - Kindness isn't grand. It's eye contact, names, follow-through.

Stay consistent - Show up even when no one is watching. Make it a habit, not a moment.

Let it ripple - Release control. Allow others to lead. Co-create what comes next.

Once you see these patterns, you start to notice them everywhere.

Leadership rarely begins with a big idea. It begins with noticing. For Dorian, it happened during the simplest conversation. When he was 12, we were driving, talking about nothing in particular, when he looked out the window and asked: *"Mom…what are the kids going to do for breakfast when school ends?"* He didn't ask it dramatically. He asked it plainly, the way a person asks a question they already know the answer to.

Summer was coming, and with it the reality that school meals would end and some kids wouldn't have breakfast. Once Dorian understood that, he couldn't look away. A few days later, we were at NextHome, my real estate brokerage office. He mentioned his cereal idea to one of the agents - not as a pitch, just as something he'd been thinking about. The agent really listened and said, *"You should come to our Humans Over Houses meeting."*

He ended up sitting at a lunch table with a group of seasoned, community - minded agents. They weren't there to humor him. They were there because they recognized what it looks like when a child genuinely sees a need.

He didn't stand up or present anything. He simply explained that he didn't want kids to go hungry during summer vacation. The idea sparked a friendly competition fueled by generosity and a shared sense of responsibility. Suddenly it wasn't just Dorian's effort anymore, it belonged to everyone in the room.

I've seen that moment before, and it moves me every time. When Dorian names a need and invites others in, something powerful happens. The work becomes collective and the energy grows. What started as one kid's concern becomes something a community works together to solve.

Creating the Conditions

Dorian had been invited to speak to a group of high school students in a local business class. He was there to share what entrepreneurship looks like from his perspective and the impact he has had on our community at such a young age.

He walked them through his slides, answered questions, and then clicked to the final slide: *"What I'm Working on Now."* It was a picture of his cereal drive and the shift in the room was instant. These students had heard how the Humans Over Houses group turned the idea into a challenge. They saw how adults leaned in. And what they recognized was something powerful: This is something we could do, too.

Hands flew up. Questions came rapid-fire and before I could fully grasp what was happening, Dorian leaned forward and said: *"Well…if your school joins the challenge, I'll throw an ice cream party for the winning classroom."*

The entire room lit up. By the end of the day, the entire school had joined the cereal challenge. And in the last week of the school year, when teens are mentally already halfway to summer, they collected three full carloads of cereal.

As Dorian walked the halls collecting boxes from classrooms, he met a teacher who paused for a moment before handing him another stack. She looked at him and said quietly, *"I grew up in foster care. I knew hunger. I wanted to help."*

A child showed up with a box. A teacher showed up with her whole story. Leadership doesn't travel downward from adult to child. It spreads outward - heart to heart, story to story, action to action.

 ## How Leadership Spreads

Consistency in a child rarely appears out of nowhere. Someone has to create the conditions where it can grow, and for me that meant treating Dorian's ideas seriously enough to build structure around them.

The meetings, emails, drop-offs, and planning were never separate from the lesson. They were part of it.

As he grew, I invited him further into the work-not just the visible parts people notice, but the pieces that make anything sustainable. Sometimes that meant sitting together at the table with a stack of receipts, entering numbers line by line and talking through where the money came from, where it went, and why every detail mattered.

It wasn't the part he enjoyed most, and it certainly wasn't the exciting side of any project, but he understood that carrying an idea all the way through means learning to walk the talk.

Leadership is not only built in the visible moments people celebrate. It is also shaped by the responsibilities that happen behind the scenes- the follow-through, the details, and the discipline that make everything else possible.

I wasn't teaching him through lectures. I was teaching through access, space, and trust. I didn't lead for him. I led with him. I made room for his leadership to take shape. That's the same philosophy I've used with my college students for years. One of them wrote during their experiential project:

"At first, I hated the idea of posting online three times a week. But the posting taught me. I collected my own data. I learned by experimenting."

Her words reminded me of Gary Vaynerchuk's core principle: *"You don't know what works until you do it."* Not plan it. Don't think about it. Do it.

James Clear calls this *"identity through repetition."*

Adam Grant calls it *"micro-courage."*

Mel Robbins calls it *"action before confidence."*

Watching my students and watching my son, I started calling it something else: The D-Max Effect. It looked like permission given early, modeled visibly, and reinforced through repetition. Action came before certainty. Kindness was practiced in ordinary moments. Consistency built trust over time. Control was released so leadership could ripple outward. Unlike most classes, there was no test waiting at the end. No single right answer to work toward. A student could earn an A and still raise no money, because the grade was never built around the outcome alone. It was built around the process. The choices they made. The conversations they initiated. The decisions they had to own when something didn't work and they needed to pivot. Leadership wasn't taught; it was built in motion, and that's exactly what I was watching in Dorian and in my students. They did not wait for a perfect idea or for the moment they felt fully ready. They simply took the first step, then the next, learning that consistency has a way of becoming credibility, credibility has a way of becoming influence, and influence, when rooted in something genuine, creates momentum.

That momentum is what turned a simple cereal drive into adults rising around a lunch table, high school students launching a school-wide challenge, entire communities joining a shared mission, and a young boy eventually being recognized by the Brewer City Council for the work he has been doing.

People do not follow talent as much as they follow patterns. What I watched in Dorian and in my students was the same thing taking shape: small acts of care repeated often enough that people began to trust what they represented.

Leadership is rarely about being extraordinary. More often, it is about being steady, showing up for something small, returning to it again and again, and allowing that rhythm to shape who you are becoming. That is how consistency begins to matter beyond the individual. It builds leaders, and over time, those leaders begin to shape the communities around them.

Every movement of change - personal, generational, or cultural - begins the same way: someone notices something, cares enough to act, and returns the next day willing to continue.

Chapter 9

D-Max Merch & The Birth of A Kid Entrepreneur

As Covid reshaped daily life, uncertainty was everywhere, but so were opportunities to step in. A local nonprofit was delivering meals to cancer patients who were isolated and immunocompromised, and they were looking for volunteers to bring groceries to people's homes.

One night, while scrolling, I came across a call for help and clicked to learn more. As I read the founder's story, my heart sank. He had started the nonprofit in his mother's honor after losing her to cancer as a teenager, turning his own loss into a way of caring for others who were walking through illness and uncertainty. That kind of story is hard to move past without feeling something. They were looking for people willing to help with deliveries, and the more I read, the more certain I felt that this was something Dorian and I should step into together. So we signed up.

Every week, we drove through neighborhoods with meals in the backseat, and Dorian carried each bag to the door. What he saw on those porches changed him and honestly, it changed me too.

There was a four-year-old boy, completely nonverbal and battling cancer, who lit up the moment he saw Dorian. There was an elderly woman who waved from her window each time, tears already in her eyes before we reached the step. And there was one patient who met us at the door for the last time, quietly telling us she did not have much longer and was leaving to spend her final days with her daughter.

For Dorian, those visits became an awakening. He saw food insecurity and loneliness. He learned that sometimes helping someone also means learning how to say goodbye. But the deeper impact was not only in what he saw. It was in what he felt, and in the conversations that followed - about sadness, about vulnerability, and about the strange truth that showing up for people can feel both heavy and deeply meaningful at the same time.

What We Were Really Learning

We were practicing emotional intelligence before we had words for it. Researchers call this co-regulation: the process of an adult helping a child navigate big feelings by naming them, normalizing them, and making space for them.

It builds three core emotional intelligence skills:

Self-awareness (*What am I feeling?*)
Empathy (*What might they be feeling?*)
Resilience (*What do I do with these feelings?*)

Emotional intelligence isn't something you teach once and check off a list. It grows when we don't rush children past their emotions and when we're willing to examine our own along the way. It isn't a milestone. It's a practice.

Daniel Goleman calls emotional intelligence the core of effective leadership and what science now confirms is something parents have always known: children grow stronger when they are allowed to feel deeply and are supported while they do. On those porches, Dorian was processing his emotions in real time, that sadness isn't something to avoid, that compassion can be a form of strength, that connection is worth the vulnerability, and that service can hold both joy and grief at once. Again and again, he saw how the smallest acts could matter the most.

Those visits were never just about delivering food. They were about connection. They showed him how one small act can change someone's day, someone's week, or sometimes someone's final season of life. Like so much of what shaped him, the lesson was not delivered all at once. It was built through repetition, through showing up, through feeling something deeply enough to carry it forward. Over time, he was learning that kindness carries weight when it is rooted in genuine awareness of what others may be carrying themselves. Kindness becomes leadership when it is sustained by empathy.

Building Something from Nothing

The idea for *D-Max Merch* didn't begin as a business plan. It began as a child's attempt to turn compassion into action and only later did the structure of a business grow around it.

He started asking questions: *"How do I tell people what I'm doing?" "How do we help even more families?"* He came up with the name. He chose the colors and fonts for his logo all while he was still in second grade, learning to read the world even as he learned to read words.

Then came the conversation every parent eventually has with a child: *"Can I have social media?"*

"Yes," I told him. *"You can have the tool - as long as you use them for good, and we do it together."*

He didn't hesitate. He picked the photos. He learned how to buy a domain. He sat beside me as we built the website together, one page at a time. He worked with a graphic designer on his logo - giving direction, choosing layouts, adjusting colors until it felt like him.

And yes, I helped. I still do. But this is his operation. Every post goes through him. We discuss the content, the message, the why behind what we share. He knows the landscape. He understands the purpose. He's not a child with a platform - he's a CEO who also happens to call me his business partner. It's the title I'm proudest of, right after Mom.

That is the part many people miss: leadership is often built in ordinary moments when children are invited into real decision - whether that means helping shape an idea, learning how to cook dinner, managing a simple task, or staying present long enough to understand that responsibility is something they grow into by being trusted with it.

Momentum Is Built Before It Is Seen

Leaders extend an invitation: *Come with me. Let's do this together.* From the beginning, that is exactly what Dorian did - and people responded.

He designed his first piece of merch in 2020 with one clear goal: sell twelve shirts - the minimum needed to make the first print run happen - with a percentage of every sale set aside to fight food insecurity. He made video after video, asking people to join him. And in the process, he learned something far more important than how to sell a shirt. He learned how to talk about what he cared about. How to look into a camera and speak with conviction. How to stay with an idea long enough for other people to believe in it too.

He got his twelve orders.

What mattered most wasn't the number. It was that he had taken the first real step.

That is why what came later never felt sudden to me. When 2025 brought one meaningful project after another - the cereal drive, the birthday cake stand, classroom visits, Badge vs. Badge softball, and the book launch - it may have looked from the outside as though everything arrived at once.

But momentum rarely begins where people first notice it.

What others were seeing in those months was the visible result of years spent practicing how to ask, how to follow up, how to communicate clearly, and how to keep showing up even when he felt tired or uncertain.

Each small effort widened his circle, because every fundraiser introduced him to new people, every collaboration taught him how to work alongside others, and every repeated act of generosity made it easier for people to say yes when the next invitation came.

Over time, that is how trust accumulated. What began as a child's simple idea slowly became something larger because people had watched him return to the work often enough to believe he would keep showing up.

That is how kindness begins to scale, how leadership grows through repetition, and how influence is built - one invitation at a time, with others choosing to step in because they understand there is room for them at the table.

One truth we do not say often enough is that meaningful change does not require everyone to stand at the front. In fact, most lasting work depends on the people who quietly choose to stand beside it. For every person who steps forward visibly, there are many others whose consistency, encouragement, and willingness to say yes are what allow the work to continue. That was true when Dorian and I delivered meals during Covid. We were not leading that mission. We simply believed in what someone else had started and chose to help carry it forward.

Leadership grows when people are invited in early, trusted with something real, and reminded that contribution does not need to be loud to matter. Dorian learned early that leadership is not about standing above anyone. It is about making room, honoring the people beside you, and understanding that meaningful work lasts longer when others know they belong there too.

The Words We Pass Down

One afternoon, we were in a second-grade classroom handing out copies of a child's book *"D-Max's Birthday Wish,"* and Dorian took his time signing each book, asking every child their name before writing something personal inside the cover.

When I leaned over his shoulder, I paused, because in his best handwriting he had written the words "Dream Big," and for a moment it caught me off guard in the best possible way. Those were the same words I used to write when signing my own book, the *Power of Transparency*, and seeing them there felt like an echo of something that had been passed down without either of us ever needing to name it.

That phrase did not begin with me. It came from the kind of family I was raised in, where dreaming big was spoken often and reinforced through the opportunities my parents worked hard to create for us. They believed in showing up, contributing, and making things better wherever they could, but they also made sure I experienced what possibility looked like firsthand through the rooms they brought me into, the people they connected me with, and the way they treated opportunity as something to step toward rather than something to fear.

Looking back, I understand how much of that shaped me. Their words mattered, but so did the way they lived. They showed me that community mattered, that relationships mattered, and that if something was worth caring about, it was worth giving your energy to. Without realizing it then, I was learning the same pattern I would later repeat with Dorian - creating space, opening doors, and trusting that proximity would teach what words alone never could.

Watching him sign his own book and write those same words made me realize how naturally those lessons continue to travel. What children witness quietly settles in long before they understand it fully, and over time those repeated examples begin to shape what they believe is possible for themselves.

That is why leadership is rarely formed through lectures and workshops alone. It grows through proximity, through repetition, and through ordinary moments returned to often enough that they begin to define how a child moves through the world. What they witness shapes what they believe, what they believe shapes what they attempt, and over time those attempts begin to shape who they become.

What struck me most in that classroom was not simply that he wrote "Dream Big," but that he did it naturally, as though those words had already become part of how he understood encouragement, possibility, and what it means to leave someone with hope.

The Social Media Shift
(& the Lesson Every Home Can Use)

One of my students once wrote something that captured exactly what happens when young people realize their voice can carry weight: *"I learned how to bring a mission to life with one simple post…and it changed the way I think about my own purpose."*

What she was describing had very little to do with social media itself. The deeper lesson was meaning - the courage to put something real into the world, allow yourself to be seen, and invite others to help solve a problem that matters. What made it powerful was learning how to use a voice with intention, something many young people are rarely invited to practice even while spending so much of life online.

Dorian learned that same lesson firsthand.

After spending the entire month of September collecting birthday cake mixes, frosting, and candles, he delivered everything to a local food pantry. They were grateful, but they were also honest. Winter was coming, and while the birthday supplies mattered, cash was what would keep the utilities covered in the harder months ahead. They also knew something important: Dorian had a way of inviting people to respond that often reached further than a single donation drive could on its own. So he set a goal to raise five hundred dollars.

What followed began with a simple post - an open invitation to our community to help meet a need that had just become clearer to him. Within a month, more than seventeen hundred dollars had come in.

That is the lesson social media kept teaching both my students and my son: when people show up authentically and invite others into something meaningful, connection often follows, and purpose begins to grow beyond the original ask.

As Rohit Bhargava writes in Likeonomics, *when you focus on meaning, you begin to understand that results are not always measured by numbers alone.* That idea has always sat underneath *D-Max Merch*, because what we were building was never simply about selling something. It was about creating a way for purpose to take shape in the real world, something that invited connection, required courage, and gave people a tangible way to participate.

What I have learned, though, is that purpose and structure have to grow together. Profit is not the enemy of generosity; it is often what allows generosity to continue. Every item carries a margin, every partnership needs thought behind it, and every fundraiser works best when there is a clear goal. Purpose without structure rarely lasts. More often, it leads to exhaustion, and I have no interest in teaching my son that constant output is something to admire. We talk openly about when it is time to pause, step back, and recharge, which is why there are seasons when our social media goes quiet after months of steady activity. The mission is still there, but so is the understanding that meaningful work has to leave room for rest, because sustainability is not only financial, it is personal too.

Chapter 10

The New Generational Wealth

Some forms of wealth are easy to measure. Others reveal themselves slowly, in the way a person handles opportunity, responds to responsibility, or instinctively makes room for others. The older I get, the more I understand that what lasts most is rarely what sits in an account. It is what lives in habits, expectations, relationships, and the belief that you can step into a room, contribute, and help build something meaningful. That is the kind of wealth I think about now, because it is the kind that keeps multiplying when it is shared.

Yes, my parents taught me to save money. They modeled discipline, responsibility, and the *save first* rule every financial planner teaches, but what stayed with me most was not the rule itself. It was the pattern behind it - the consistency of watching adults make thoughtful choices, plan ahead, and treat stability as something worth protecting. They invested deeply in education, and in creating a home where structure and responsibility were simply part of daily life. Raising four children required intention, and they carried that responsibility steadily enough that when my father became ill and had to retire far earlier than anyone expected, the foundation beneath our family held. It was not easy, but it was steady because they had built a life disciplined enough to absorb change without collapsing under it.

That is the kind of wealth I understand more clearly now. It is built brick by brick, habit by habit, lesson by lesson, and often goes unnoticed while you are living inside it because repetition rarely announces itself while it is shaping you. Only later do you realize those patterns became part of how you move through the world, what you trust, and what you begin passing forward without even realizing it. There comes a point when every adult has the opportunity to ask what kind of steadiness, what kind of possibility, and what kind of example the people closest to them are absorbing simply by watching how they live.

Stay Long Enough to Learn

Looking back now, I can see the rhythm beneath so many of their decisions: have a plan, and if the plan no longer fits, do not abandon it too quickly. Stay with it long enough to learn something before deciding what comes next.

What they were teaching was more than discipline. It was how to move through uncertainty without reacting too early, how to gather information before deciding, how to tolerate discomfort long enough to understand whether you are growing or simply in the wrong place. That pattern stayed with me after college, when I was accepted into a graduate program in Boston.

I had never lived in a city before, but I said yes anyway because that was the lesson I had absorbed: gather the information, try the thing, commit before deciding what the experience means.

For a full semester, I stayed with it. I adjusted to city life, pushed through the discomfort, and learned what commitment feels like. And then, slowly, clarity arrived. I was not simply stretched by something new; I was deeply unhappy. The program was intensely competitive, and the future it pointed toward did not match the life I wanted to build back in Maine. Walking away was not impulsive and came with a lot of internal struggle. It meant finishing the semester, having hard conversations, and being honest enough to separate discomfort from misalignment. My parents stood beside me through that process, even helping me untangle a lease when it became clear I needed to come home. Their support did not remove the lesson. It strengthened it, because what they modeled was not blind endurance. They showed me how to leave something thoughtfully after learning what it had come to teach. That understanding became part of how I later guided Dorian.

When he was four, he announced that he wanted to do gymnastics, so we signed him up. For two weeks he moved through the house like pure momentum, flipping, cartwheeling, and talking about little else. Then, just as quickly, he decided he was done. When he told me he wanted to quit, I reminded him that making a choice also means honoring the commitment attached to it. He did not have to sign up again after the session ended, but he did need to finish what he had started, because the lesson was never gymnastics itself. It was learning how to stay long enough to understand his own decision. He finished the session and never returned, but what stayed was something more useful than any single activity: the understanding that follow-through builds self-trust, and that sometimes the clearest decisions come after you have remained long enough to know why you are making them.

There is another layer to generational wealth that rarely gets named, even though it shapes a person long before they understand its value: social capital. It is built through relation- ships, trust, familiarity, and the confidence that comes from being invited close enough to watch how connection works.

I think about that often when I see what happens after young people are given early exposure to real rooms and real conver- sations. I tell my students - and really anyone I mentor - that they are always welcome to stay in touch, because sometimes what matters most is knowing the relationship does not end when the class, program, or project does. One of the clearest examples came from a student I met during his freshman year in one of my business classes. He stood out immediately - curious, thoughtful, and clearly wired to build. Three years later, he reached out to tell me he had launched his business and was looking for ways to meet more people. He had taken me up on something many people hear but do not always use: the invitation to reconnect.

So I invited him to be my guest at a chamber event, introduced him around the room, and made sure he left with business cards in his pocket and new names in his phone. What mattered most was not the event itself, but that he began to experience what happens when someone enters a room prepared to connect rather than simply observe. That is the invisible currency many people do not realize they are receiving when someone opens a door and stays beside them long enough for the room to feel navigable.

I understand that even more clearly now because I can watch a similar confidence forming in Dorian. He knows how to speak to adults with respect and clarity, how to enter a room without shrinking, and how to understand that collaboration is not accidental but something people build deliberately over time. He has engaged in enough conversations, enough partnerships, and enough moments of generosity that community now feels natural to him.

As Robert Putnam writes, social capital is the glue that holds society together, but what *matters* to me is how early that glue begins to form. That is why these early experiences matter so much. When children watch generosity move through a community, they learn that asking for help is not weakness. When they see collaboration modeled, they understand they do not have to build everything alone. When they are treated as though they belong, they begin carrying that belief into every room that follows.

Discipline, reputation, effort, and leadership all grow stronger when they begin early and are repeated consistently.

That same pattern is visible far beyond finances. One invitation, one room, one early responsibility often becomes something larger later because confidence grows the same way compound interest does - slowly at first, and then all at once.

The D-Max Effect

Chapter 11

Raising A Leader
While Becoming One

In 2018, I was the commencement speaker at the University of Maine Graduate School. My family sat in the President's Box, and I remember looking out at the crowd and offering a simple message: Be limitless. It wasn't a slogan. It was survival. That phrase had carried me through some of my lowest seasons, reminding me that who I was becoming mattered more than where I had been. I wanted the audience-new graduates and parents alike-to hear this clearly: Life isn't meant to be lived on autopilot. There was a season, especially during my divorce and the move back to my hometown, when life felt full of decisions I had never planned to make and emotions I had no choice but to move through. From the outside, it may have looked like constant change, but beneath each shift was the same quiet question I kept returning to: *Is this moving me toward a life that feels more honest, more grounded, and ultimately more whole?* When the answer was no, I learned to adjust course.

After my speech, I caught Dorian's eye. He was beaming

- proud of his mom. Years later, I felt that same pride standing and watching him step onto the field at the Little League World Series. This time there was no speech and no microphone, only a first pitch thrown in front of thousands as he was recognized as a community hero. One out of 5 in the country - the only kid. The roles had shifted, but the feeling had not.

A similar moment happened recently when Dorian was invited to do his first on-air interview. It took place in the same studio where, more than a decade earlier, I had once done a segment on coworking. What he did not remember until I reminded him was that he had already been there.

It was the Fourth of July. His daycare was closed, so he came with me. During the segment, he wandered around the set while I kept talking, smiling on the outside and quietly hoping he would not derail the moment.

Now years later, he was the one on camera - calm, confident, ready - while I stood off-screen.

That role reversal, in that same space, made visible something I have come to believe deeply: when children are invited into real work, real conversations, and real community often enough, they begin to carry themselves as though they belong there.

Dorian has been part of Kiwanis International for years. They have supported his fundraisers, watched him grow, and shown up often enough that encouragement became something steady rather than occasional. Recently, one of the members and I were scrolling through old photos and found one from his ninth birthday, taken at a meeting where they surprised him with a celebration, gave him the floor to speak, and then helped him reach the goal he had set.

That is what repeated support makes possible. Long before a child steps into a moment that feels big, they are shaped by smaller moments where people make space for them, listen seriously, and stay nearby while they learn what it feels like to speak, try, and keep going even when nerves are present.

What being part of Kiwanis International has given him is repeated practice. They let him speak, trust him with attention and showing him that courage does not mean the absence of fear—it means learning that you can move forward while people who believe in you are still in the room.

At the Little League World Series, just before he stepped onto the field to accept his award and throw the first pitch, he stood quietly, shoulders back, taking it all in.

"Are you nervous?" I whispered.

He paused. *"Yeah. I'm really nervous. Do you see how many people are here? And I have to throw a pitch."*

To him, the fear was real, but so was everything that had prepared him for that moment. Courage had already been practiced many times in smaller rooms, with smaller audiences, and with people who had spent years quietly helping him believe he could step forward anyway. His courage strengthened mine. When my own confidence wavers, I think of him stepping forward, and I keep going.

Motherhood. Leadership. Reinvention.

Motherhood, leadership, and reinvention often arrived in the same season, asking for adjustments before I felt fully ready. As a single mother, that adjustment carried a deeper question beneath everything else: *Who am I now?* Around that time, I met Hugh, the kind of mentor who did not offer comfort for its own sake, but a perspective strong enough to steady you when your own thinking felt uncertain. We stayed in touch for more than a decade, and during many of my rebuilding years he became one of those steady voices who believed in my future when my own confidence was still catching up. He often saw possibility more clearly than I did. Sitting across from my mentor with a beer in his hand, he looked me in the eyes and said, *"You don't need permission. Be seen. Be big. Go and do NOT take your foot off the gas!"* That moment stayed with me! Permission to keep moving forward, even when the path wasn't perfectly clear. Don't do everything but focus on what matters, fully, honestly, and without waiting for someone else to tell you it's okay to begin.

Years later, when I invited him to speak at a conference I was hosting, one of the first things he asked was whether Dorian would be there. I told him I had not given it much thought, and without hesitation he said, *"He needs to be in the room."*

The certainty of it stayed with me, and so did something else: relationships only deepen when someone follows through after the first conversation. Hugh had once said stay in touch, and I did. That simple choice created space for encouragement, perspective, and honesty through many seasons of my life. Some people pass through your life briefly. Others say something that keeps echoing long enough to change how you move through your own.

Chapter 12

What Happens
When One Child Shows Up

By the time Dorian was thirteen, I started to notice a pattern in the way adults responded to him. Some had seen him organizing fundraisers or talking about kids going hungry with a clarity far beyond his years. Others had watched him in more ordinary places - on the ballfield, in practice, in the moments between plays.

One of those adults was a local business owner who had spent years coaching baseball in the community and had built a small business around something he loved: Maine specialty items, the kind of products that tell the story of a place. He'd seen Dorian play - not just how he hit or fielded, but how he carried himself. The focus. The accountability. The way he showed up.

So when that same business owner later came across Dorian's community work - the posts, the fundraisers, the open invitations to help - it didn't feel surprising. It felt familiar. He already knew who Dorian was.

That's the thing about kids who are given room to lead early: their character doesn't switch on for special occasions. It shows up everywhere.

"I just saw what they were doing, and I couldn't just sit back and watch," he said later. *"I was like, 'I want to partner up with these guys.'"*

That sentence matters more than it seems. I couldn't just sit back and watch.

That's how momentum really begins - not with spotlight moments, when someone choosing to step in and say: I see you. Let's build this together.

Throughout the busiest month of the year, a $1.00 from every gift box sold would go directly to keeping the local food pantry stocked - helping families at the exact moment demand peaks. When Dorian was asked why this mattered to him, his answer was simple.

"Everybody needs food; everybody deserves food," he said. *"So we're really trying to push to make an impact and help people out."*

In addition to working together to donate to the local food pantry, they also created something more personal - a specialty box tied directly to Dorian's work, with half of the proceeds supporting kids who rely on school snacks to get through the day. It was a natural fit: a business built around Maine's story, partnering with a kid writing a new chapter in it.

A child brings heart and clarity. An adult brings perspective and infrastructure. Trust does the rest. The D-Max Effect isn't about kids doing adult work, and it's not about adults taking over. It's about seeing leadership in a child - on the field, in the community, in the moments - and saying: I see this. I believe in it. And I can help.

That lesson stays with a child far longer than any scoreboard or fundraiser ever could. Once a kid learns that who they are matters - everywhere they show up - they carry that confidence. And that recognition didn't stop at the edges of our community.

When the Story Traveled 

During Dorian's first birthday cake fundraiser, a local news story was shared more widely than we ever expected. Messages arrived first, then cards and handwritten letters from people we had never met. One woman from out of state wrote after seeing the story:

"It is a wonderful thing you are doing for people! You are a very special person. Nowadays it is rare for someone your age to be so thoughtful. In life we get back for the things we do. Remember these words as you get older. I wish you a wonderful life full of adventures."

Another letter arrived from a retired Marine on the West Coast. Inside was a check and a simple note:

"I saw your story on the news. I thought your efforts should be rewarded. I am enclosing a check for $100 to help with your birthday cake giveaway. Keep up the good work."

What moved me most was strangers who didn't even live near us took the time to put encouragement into writing, creating something tangible we still have today. At the time, neither of us fully understood how lasting that would feel, but those cards became reminders that kindness often reaches farther than the moment in which it begins. These were not people looking for recognition, and they were not connected to the community this fundraiser was serving. They simply saw a child leading with heart and chose to answer it with generosity of their own.

Chapter 13

When One Kid Moves,
A Community Responds

This chapter is really about how leadership spreads sideways, often in moments adults almost miss. I saw it clearly one summer evening in a hockey locker room, just after Dorian had returned from the Little League World Series, an experience most kids only dream about. After practice, still half in gear, he sat with his teammates talking the way kids do when something has genuinely excited them, replaying what it felt like to be there, what the field looked like, how big everything felt, and what it was like to stand in a place he had only ever seen on television. Later that night, one of the moms reached out to tell me her son had come home buzzing. He could not stop talking about it. Dorian had been to the Little League World Series, had thrown out the first pitch, and now he wanted that too.

Then she asked the question that stayed with me: *"Do you think he knows what Dorian did to get there?"*

Because none of what had led to that moment had come up in the locker room, not the fundraisers, not the community work, not the years of showing up long before anyone outside our town was paying attention.

And that is often how influence works. Children notice what feels possible before they understand what built it, and sometimes the most powerful thing they can witness is simply another child who has been close enough to effort, consistency, and purpose that it begins to look natural.

People had been watching for years: consistency is hard to ignore. He had support - a growing circle of adults and kids cheering him on. He was responding to what he could see, one moment at a time, and over time that made other people begin imagining what might also be possible for them.

What people responded to was the sincerity underneath it.

What struck me most was what happened next. The conversation didn't end with admiration. It shifted into action. Her son wasn't just inspired by the story - he was curious about the path.

So I offered the simplest advice I know to be true: Ask him what he's passionate about. Then go do that. Follow their lead. The Little League World Series wasn't just a dream that came true for Dorian. It became proof that dreams are built, not handed out, and that's the kind of truth kids can carry without being burdened by it.

Dorian didn't chase that dream alone. He chased it with his community and that's the part we often miss. I could feel the invisible threads- the quiet connections woven over years of showing up, following through, and doing good without a script. None of those moments were isolated. Each one pulled gently on the next, creating a network strong enough to carry a dream all the way to that field.

This is the D-Max Effect at work: when kids act with sincerity, communities respond with trust, and over time that trust creates momentum. Dreams rarely come to life in isolation; they take shape through relationships, through service, through effort repeated often enough that other people begin to step in alongside them.

What begins with one child noticing often grows because others choose to pay attention. Inspiration gains strength when it is matched by consistency, kids lead, adults support, communities respond, and before long the pattern begins repeating itself in ways no one fully planned.

I saw it again through Brewer Youth Football.

Dorian has never played football, but he loves the program and has long treated Brewer Youth Football as part of his community. He stops by practices, cheers from the sidelines at games, knows the coaches, knows the kids, and moves through that space with the same ease he carries in places where relationships have been built over time, because to him community is never defined only by where you officially belong, but by where you consistently show up.

And Brewer Youth Football has always shown up for him too. When he decided to run a cereal drive for the local food pantry, that relationship became visible in a way that stayed with me. A carload of cereal arrived, and when he began talking calmly and clearly about how food pantries really work, explaining that donated food matters but cash is what keeps the shelves stocked and the lights on, Venmo notifications from families connected to the program started appearing one after another. There was no pressure and no performance in it, only people responding because they understood the need and trusted the kid explaining it. What moved me most was how naturally that trust had formed, not through one big moment, but through many smaller ones that had taught people he meant what he said. Their response gave him more than support for the fundraiser; it gave him the feeling of **being fully seen inside a community he already cared about, a reminder that when circles begin to overlap, a child starts to understand how much strength there is in belonging to something larger than himself.**

Relationships built over time begin to move on their own. Leadership stops looking like authority and starts looking like care. In locker rooms. On sidelines. In kitchens and parking lots. In conversations where a parent chooses to say, *"I know how to help-let's do this together."* That's the invitation I want to leave you with.

If a child in your life comes home inspired by someone else's story, don't rush to explain it away. Don't shrink the dream to something safer or smaller. Ask them what they care about. Ask them what they want to try and then walk beside them while they figure it out.

And if you see a cause that matters-one you want to get behind-invite a child into it. Let them help shape the effort. Let them understand the why. Let them be part of the work, not just the outcome. That's what happens when programs like Brewer Youth Football show up-not because they're asked, but because they care. Adults lead with resources. Kids learn what it looks like to respond. And together, something stronger forms.

Because the dream that came true for Dorian isn't meant to be admired from afar. It's meant to be chased- by your child, in your community, starting exactly where you are. One kid moves. An adult joins. A community responds. And everyone becomes stronger in the process.

The D-Max Effect

Chapter 14

The Pause I Didn't Plan For

You've probably spotted a few rough edges in these pages. A sentence that could have used one more pass. A paragraph that might have been tightened if I had given it another week. You'd be right. I chose to let them stay because this book was written inside a narrow window of time, and some things mattered more than perfect polish.

On January 1, I lost one of the roles that had provided steady income and health insurance- the kind of practical stability you do not fully appreciate until it is suddenly removed. I was not without work. I still had other income streams, other responsibilities, and other pieces of my life already in motion. But anyone who has built a life across multiple lanes understands that not all income carries the same weight. Some pay bills. Some offer flexibility. Some hold the safety net together.

This loss changed the equation immediately.

I was still standing, but one of the beams had been removed, and you feel that right away. There is something disorienting about beginning a new year with uncertainty when everyone around you is talking about goals, momentum, and fresh starts. One conversation, one shift, and suddenly the structure of your days looks different. What you assumed would continue no longer belongs to you in the same way.

After the initial sting settled, another truth began to surface: the pause I had not chosen might be exactly what I needed.

For six years, The *D-Max Effect* had existed as a living document - unfinished, growing, waiting. A messy Google Doc filled with stories, observations, quotes from people who shaped me, lessons gathered while building businesses, raising my son, navigating reinvention, and learning how often life asks you to rebuild while still moving. I returned to it often, usually with conviction, then set it aside whenever life became too full or too demanding.

This time, I could not set it aside. I had given myself a deadline that carried more weight than any publishing calendar: March 18, my father's birthday. That left just a few months to refine every chapter. Not endless time to revisit every sentence until it felt complete. Just enough time to decide that honesty, finishing, and meaning mattered more than perfection. It needed to be in the world.

My father understood what it meant to show up fully. He understood responsibility, leadership, and the kind of steadiness people build their lives around without always realizing how deeply it shapes them until much later. Publishing this book on his birthday was not symbolism for symbolism's sake. It was finishing something in the spirit of someone who taught me that when something matters, you do not wait for ideal conditions. You keep moving. Here I am.

Some days with clarity. Some days carrying disappointment. Some days wondering whether uncertainty, ambition, memory, and hope could all sit at the same table without pulling against one another. They can. Somewhere inside that compressed timeline, I understood something I had written about many times but had not yet fully tested in this exact way: resilience rarely arrives looking inspiring while you are living it. More often, it looks unfinished. Slightly uncertain. Full of questions. Still moving anyway. It was the same lesson I had spent years teaching Dorian: take what is in front of you, decide what matters, and build forward from there.

Around that same time, I got an email from the Boys & Girls Club.

"Hi Lisa-many years ago, we received a very large donation of stuffed bears, which we turned into 'Birthday Bears.' On every Club member's birthday, they got to pick out a stuffed bear to take home. It became something many kids looked forward to - knowing that every child was getting at least one gift on their birthday.

A little over a year ago, we finally ran out of bears and had to part ways with the tradition. I was wondering if this is something D-Max would be interested in helping us get up and running again."

Dorian and I went to work. He presented at civic organizations, partnered with high school athletics, and set up collection points on a youth night. Bears started arriving one by one, then in batches, then in carloads.

Some people told me this was the season to say no - that I should narrow my focus, protect my time, and concentrate only on replacing the income I had lost. They were not wrong. They were just measuring success differently than I was at that moment.

Because what I was learning, again, is that life is rarely as binary as people make it sound. It is not always *either solve your own problems or show up for someone else.* Sometimes both belong in the same season. Sometimes the very act of giving is what steadies you enough to keep facing what is uncertain. When we dropped off the first batch of bears, we watched children light up as they chose one for their birthday.

Then something else happened. A little girl we had met during a classroom visit arrived carrying two bags of stuffed animals. She handed them over proudly, as if she already understood she was contributing to something larger than herself. Later, her mother sent me a note. In the car afterward, her daughter had said, *"This is so much fun."* That small sentence stayed with me because it captured something adults often forget: when children are truly invited into purpose, giving does not feel heavy. Leadership does not feel intimidating. It feels exciting. It feels possible. It feels like something they can own.

Her mother added that she now wanted to help every month and was already thinking about how to support their local shelter next. This little girl is one example, but she represents something I have seen again and again: when kids are trusted with meaning, they rise to meet it. When they understand their actions matter, they want more responsibility, not less. Kindness becomes contagious - not because anyone forces it, but because purpose expands people.

And that same principle applies to adults.

It would have been easy to sit at my computer and let stress narrow everything - to replay worst-case scenarios, stare at spreadsheets, and measure my worth by what felt uncertain. I did some of that too. I am human. But every time we showed up - every time a child picked out a bear, every time a parent sent a note, every time generosity moved outward and then circled back - I was reminded that my own life was still larger than the problem directly in front of me.

Perspective has a way of doing that. Giving did not distract me from reality. It grounded me in it. It reminded me that scarcity is often loudest when we forget how much still exists beyond our immediate fear. That even while one part of life feels unstable, another part can still be deeply meaningful. That there can be loss and contribution. Uncertainty and generosity. Pressure and purpose. That is what this season taught me: sometimes the most useful thing you can do when life feels uncertain is not to shrink, but to stay connected to what still matters.

Take what is in front of you. Decide what matters. Build forward from there.

If this book offers anything, I hope it reminds you that agency is not loud. More often, it is practiced quietly, in choices that may not make sense to everyone else but still feel deeply right to you. I have learned that some of the most important decisions in my life have looked impractical to other people.

Over the years, people have questioned how I spend my time, why I show up the way I do, why I invest deeply in things that do not always come with a clear return. The answer is simple: the most important choices are rarely made for convenience. They are made in alignment with what matters, trusting that not everything valuable reveals its return right away - some of it arrives later, in trust, in memory, in confidence, and in the shaping of a life. Once you know what matters, the decision becomes easier to stand behind. Sometimes the return appears generations later, when you recognize in yourself - and in your child - the quiet influence of someone who taught you how to live before you fully understood what you were learning.

Chapter 15

This Is Not His
Story Or Mine - It's Ours

In Maine, one in five children goes to bed not knowing if there will be enough food tomorrow. Across the country, families are stretched thin-financially, emotionally, spiritually. We talk endlessly about solutions. We debate policy. We host panels and write plans. And yet, some of the most effective leaders responding to these challenges aren't sitting at conference tables. They're standing behind lemonade stands. This chapter begins in a small town in Maine, but it doesn't end there.

For the past six years, my son Dorian, better known in our community as D-Max, has been seeing a problem, believing he can help, and taking action. He started with a simple lemonade stand. No mission statement. No nonprofit paperwork. Just a kid, a folding table, and a belief that if people were hungry, someone should do something. So he did. That lemonade stand grew into an apple cider pop-up at a local grocer, hot cocoa fundraisers, snack drives, and partnerships with local businesses. By the time he reached middle school, Dorian had raised thousands of dollars for food pantries, youth sports programs, and families facing crisis-many of them right in his own neighborhood.

But this isn't a story about a "remarkable child." It's a case study in what happens when a child is allowed to lead and when a community chooses belief over doubt. We love to say that children are "the leaders of tomorrow." It sounds hopeful. It also lets us off the hook. In my experience, kids aren't waiting for tomorrow-they're leading today. They are doing it with a clarity adults often lose. When kids see hunger, they don't argue about logistics. They don't ask if they're qualified. They don't wait to be invited. They see something wrong and they want to make it right.

When Dorian learned that families in our area were struggling to put food on the table, he didn't ask whether he had influence or credentials. He asked one simple question: *"Where can I set up?"* Neighbors donated. Businesses partnered. Teachers shared his posts. Community members stopped by with encouragement and spare change because his intention was pure.

I see this pattern repeat itself everywhere Dorian goes - especially in classrooms. During one school visit, he shared that one of his first fundraisers was a lemonade stand he ran with his grandfather. Before he could finish the sentence, hands shot up around the room. Kids started chiming in-lemonade stands, bake sales, helping neighbors, raising money for causes they cared about. The energy in the room shifted. It wasn't a lesson being delivered from the front of the classroom anymore. It was a moment of recognition. They weren't listening to a speaker.

They were comparing notes.

You could see it on their faces-the pride, the surprise, the quiet realization that they weren't too young to make a difference. Their ideas already mattered. Their actions already counted. That spark-that instant where a child sees themselves not as a helper-in-training, but as a leader right now-is something special to witness. And it happens the moment an adult makes room for it.

What I've learned through watching this unfold is:

Kids lead with heart.
Adults lead with strategy.
Communities thrive when we make room for both.

I've seen this not only as a parent, but as an educator. During my years teaching in higher education, students consistently rose beyond expectations when they were trusted with real responsibility and encouraged to work on problems that mattered to them personally. Permission plus purpose equals performance.

The same principle applies to children.

When young people are trusted - truly trusted - with meaningful action, they rise to it. Every single time. And this isn't just inspiring. It's strategic.

Communities that engage young people meaningfully are safer, more connected, and more resilient. Volunteerism increases. Schools strengthen. Local businesses gain a generation of problem-solvers who lead with empathy and initiative. Empowering kids isn't a feel-good gesture. According to Gallup,

"79% of youth volunteers report feeling more connected to their communities through service." It's a community development strategy with long-term returns.

 ## Do What Matters

People sometimes look at my life and ask, *"How do you manage it all?"* The multiple jobs, the community commitments, the late nights and early mornings - the constant motion! The truth is, I choose what matters, and I build everything else around those choices.

Most seasons have meant working multiple jobs, and I want to be honest about that because it isn't always easy. There are days when the calendar feels relentless and mornings that begin before I feel ready, but I'm an entrepreneur raising an entrepreneur, and this is the life we've intentionally built together. It creates the flexibility and ownership that allow us to say yes when something truly matters. This isn't about chasing busyness; it's about designing a life that works for us in real time, not just on paper.

I've learned, sometimes the hard way, that you can't pour from an empty cup and you certainly can't pour when you're disconnected from what fills you. So I work in the margins: before sunrise, after bedtime, and in the spaces between meetings. Scott often takes the lead on baseball practices and games so I can sit at board tables and keep building the work we believe in, a partnership that doesn't need much explanation but makes everything possible. And those early 7 a.m. meetings? They're a lot more fun when there are donuts- just ask Dorian, who measures the success of any morning by whether frosting is involved.

As the years pass, I see the invisible threads more clearly: my father's steady leadership, my mother's strength, the mentors who invested in me before I fully understood my own potential, the teachers and colleagues who opened doors and said, *"Come with us."* Now I watch my son step into his own voice, reminding entire classrooms that leadership doesn't belong to a title or an age- it belongs to anyone willing to care enough to act.

None of this has been accidental, and none of it has been effortless. It has been built slowly, through moments of discipline and rest, courage and doubt, and the kind of love that isn't loud but lasts longer than applause ever could. I'm not doing everything; I'm doing what matters, and I'm doing it from a life shaped intentionally, one decision at a time.

If you need proof that I am far from perfect, here it is: when we wrote *"D-Max's Birthday Wish,"* I could not figure out how to get the margins right. The formatting nearly broke me. I watched tutorials, tried every workaround, and still ended up with pages that weren't flawless. But the book exists. Kids hold it in their hands. It's read at bedtime and in classrooms. Along the way I accepted that done, even imperfectly, moves the work forward in a way perfection never can.

If there is one thing I hope you take from this chapter, it's that leadership doesn't begin with certainty - it begins with action. You don't need a title to lead, and you don't need permission to start. You only need to notice what matters and take the next small step toward it, trusting that momentum builds in ways you may not recognize right away.

Chapter 16

Learning
It Together

Dorian had already run a few fundraisers when another homeschooling dad reached out. He admired what Dorian was doing and wanted his own son to experience something similar - not just entrepreneurship in theory, but the process of taking an idea, building it, and watching it become real. The boys decided to create a custom sweatshirt, starting with their own artwork. They sat with a graphic designer and watched rough sketches become print-ready files, talking through wholesale pricing, margins, and what it actually means to build something from the ground up.

From the beginning, they were clear about why they were doing it: they wanted to help a local shelter. That clarity mattered more than people often realize. Kids do better when the purpose is visible. When they understand why something exists, effort becomes easier to sustain because the work is connected to something beyond themselves. With the goal set, they mapped out a commercial - storyboards, video shoots, conversations about who they wanted involved. The adults stepped back enough for them to move.

That is the part many people miss.

Children do not need adults to control every detail. They need adults willing to provide a frame strong enough to hold the experience, while leaving enough room for real ownership inside it. The sweatshirt itself was never the main point. What mattered was what happened around it: one idea sparked another, confidence expanded, and two boys began to understand that they were capable of carrying something all the way through.

This is one of the simplest leadership patterns I have seen repeated over and over again: when young people are trusted with meaningful responsibility, they almost always rise further than adults expect. Around that same time, that same momentum spilled into something bigger. The boys launched a podcast called *Sports, Gaming, and Giving*. What began as a shared interest quickly became another layer of learning. They researched guests, learned their stories, shaped thoughtful questions, recorded, edited, published, and then showed up to do it all again.

What looked simple from the outside required discipline underneath. Again, the same framework applied: adults offered support, but not control. One of the co-hosts was a parent. He brought credibility, calm, and an unwavering belief in following kids' interests without steering them too tightly. That distinction matters. Support is not the same as takeover. The goal is not to build something polished for kids. The goal is to let them build something real enough that the learning belongs to them.

I had the privilege of being a guest on their podcast, and Dorian gave me the sweetest introduction—a kid proud of his mother in a way only a child can be when he feels ownership of the room he helped create. We talked about experiential learning: how children do not develop confidence by watching adults perform well. They develop it by participating before they feel fully ready. That conversation confirmed something I have come to believe deeply: the framework in this book works because it is not abstract. It is simple enough to repeat anywhere:

- **Offer structure.**
- **Name the purpose.**
- **Let them carry real responsibility.**
- **Stay close enough to support, but far enough back that the work becomes theirs.**

That is how confidence forms. That is how voice develops. That is how leadership begins - long before anyone calls it leadership. What these boys were really learning had very little to do with sweatshirts or microphones. They were learning how to trust themselves enough to begin.

Leveling Up to the Pros

Showing up rarely looks dramatic, but it ripples more than people realize. Sometimes it is simply standing in the bleachers at a rec or high school game, cheering on the athletes. Long before championships, recognition, or larger crowds, there is something deeply formative about being supported while growth is still underway. Kids feel that immediately. They notice who comes. They notice who stays. They respond to being seen before the outcome is impressive enough to attract attention on its own. What makes that powerful is that the principle extends far beyond sports. People grow differently when someone believes in them early.

I see it with Dorian every season. Even at thirteen, he lights up when other kids line the tunnel and cheer as players come off the ice. The shift is immediate - energy rises, confidence sharpens, belonging becomes visible. That kind of encouragement is easy to dismiss because it looks small from the outside, but it isn't. Culture is built through repeated moments like that, where people learn they matter before they have fully proven themselves.

The same pattern appears everywhere: in college students balancing academics and athletics, in children presenting ideas aloud for the first time, in young people trying something difficult before they know whether they will succeed.

Support often arrives before confidence does. It begins in ordinary moments, when someone chooses to be present while another person is still learning, still uncertain, still developing into who they may become. The things that eventually reach another level usually do so because someone stayed close enough to believe in their early stages. Children expand inside that kind of environment. So do adults. So do communities.

Over time, I have come to see that devotion is less about attachment to one outcome and more about staying engaged in a process that unfolds slowly. Progress shifts. Interests change. Plans evolve. What remains constant is the willingness to keep offering opportunities, and paying attention, adjusting course. Research from the University of Virginia found that confidence and sense of belonging commonly declines during middle school years, even while students continue learning and developing. Growth is often happening long before it becomes visible. That kind of patience changes both sides of the relationship.

Peer to Peer

One of the most powerful shifts I've watched in Dorian's leadership is when it stopped being about helping kids and started being with them. D-Max doesn't stand in front of kids his age explaining what to do. He shows up as one of them. He has become a familiar friend at the Boys & Girls Clubs of America - a place he has loved and returned to for years. He has brought his merch, frisbees and stickers to share, occasionally surprising the kids with ice cream or hot cocoa. Mostly, he comes to play, laugh, and step naturally into the energy already in the room.

When he walks through the doors, faces light up because their friend has arrived. At times, he brings another friend with him - one more kid learning what it feels like to give, to participate, and to belong to something larger than themselves. Without forcing it, Dorian expands the circle every time he does this. He is introducing the mission of the Club through presence, not explanation.

That is peer-to-peer leadership in its clearest form: kids learn from each other. They watch more closely, trust more quickly, and respond differently when leadership feels less like instruction and more like joy, generosity, and belonging.

Research has shown that adolescents are deeply shaped by peer modeling and social belonging, often responding more strongly to what they observe from trusted peers than what they are told by adults.

Chapter 17

The Adults
Who Said Yes

As another year came to a close, Dorian and I sat down to sign Christmas cards. When we stacked them up, we were shocked. There were more than forty cards: banks, schools, city government, first responders, and local organizations. These were the larger community partners - the businesses, institutions, and civic groups that had sponsored events, partnered on fundraisers, opened doors, shared platforms, and said yes to a kid with an idea and a big heart. That count did not even include the many individual donations that had come in along the way - people sending support, buying something small, contributing because they believed in what he was building.

By then, it was clear that each yes had made the next one easier. Trust compounds. A child who shows up consistently, follows through, and thanks people will eventually draws responses not only to the project in front of them, but to the character people have watched take shape over time.

That mattered, because Dorian was already thinking about what he wanted his final Little League season to look like. He was clear about one thing: he wanted to go out big.

The year before, he had raised money to purchase a new sound system for the field because he wanted players to have good "sounding" walk-up music. He wanted kids to feel seen when they stepped up to the plate. That same instinct carried into his final season when he decided to host a Badge vs. Badge softball game: Brewer Police Department versus Brewer Fire Department.

Once again, the adults said yes. The departments were generous with their time and presence. A trophy was made. Food trucks arrived. A 50/50 raffle took shape. Kids ran everywhere. People gathered along the sidelines. The concession stand buzzed with activity. It felt less like an event and more like a town recognizing itself in something simple and good.

At one point, I spoke with a first responder who had just come off the field. He told me he hadn't played on this baseball field in decades. Being out there again brought him right back to his childhood-simpler times, playing for the love of the game. This wasn't just a fundraiser, though it raised meaningful money. It was civic unity. Memory and meaning stitched together by a kid who asked and adults who followed his lead. That's the power of first responders saying yes to a child. Not just supporting an event but modeling partnership, trust, and shared pride.

The same pattern showed up again with Dorian's Birthday Cake Fundraiser. In its second year, Dorian wanted to expand the impact and knew he couldn't do it alone. So he asked for help and once again, adults said yes. He partnered with Maine Savings Federal Credit Union, placing donation boxes in branches across the state. The ask expanded beyond Dorian himself into a shared mission. Businesses were tagged. Communities were invited in. The fundraiser became something people could belong to. Even Miss Maine helped amplify the effort. By sharing her donation from a Maine Savings branch and tagging his *"D-Max Merch"* Facebook page, she extended the reach of the mission and brought visibility to the cause. What struck me most wasn't the scale, it was how naturally it grew. Not because of marketing, but because people connected with the why. Hunger isn't just about food. It's about feeling forgotten.

One day, we received a handwritten thank you card from Harvest Chapel. Inside, Pastor Gary wrote:

"Families who feel forgotten will now have birthday cakes because of YOU. Kindness like this changes everything for the people we care about. Already thinking about how we can make next year even bigger."

I held that note for a long time. Handwritten words have a way of doing that. They humanize impact we don't always get to see. They restore dignity to conversations too often flattened into numbers and logistics.

Dignity is a leadership value.

What this chapter really honors is that none of this happened because one kid was extraordinary. It happened because adults chose to say yes. They followed a child's lead. They shared power. They trusted the process.

They also did something just as important, they let Dorian feel seen. They created space for him to feel connected, valued, and part of something bigger than himself. That kind of support doesn't just celebrate a moment; it builds confidence that lasts. It tells a young person their voice matters, their ideas belong, and their dreams are worth investing in.

When a child knows there are people and organizations standing behind them- ready to show up, to believe, to help carry the vision forward - dreaming bigger stops feeling impossible. It starts feeling real.

What I have learned over time is that this does not stop mattering when childhood ends. Adults need it too. Most recently, after hosting an entrepreneurial conference, I stayed behind as the room emptied. Chairs were getting put away and tables were being cleared. The energy had settled. The space was quiet again. I noticed a small note left behind. Simple. Unassuming. *Thank you, Lisa. Physically. Mentally. Professionally.*

I stood there longer than I expected to. That note now has a permanent place on my desk. It serves as a powerful reminder that the question I always ask myself: *Am I really making a difference? The answer is yes.* It's just hard to measure. It shows up as breadcrumbs: a handwritten note, a remembered moment, a quiet sign that something truly landed. Sometimes, that's enough to keep going.

Maybe the invitation isn't to wait until you feel certain you're on the right path. Maybe it's to become part of someone else's breadcrumbs: a quick text, a small moment of acknowledgment, a note left for someone you admire. The kind of gesture that lets another person feel seen and reminds them they're not walking alone. Because none of us really find the trail by ourselves - we build it together, one conversation at a time.

Chapter 18

When Impact Becomes Tangible

One afternoon, a post appeared on a community page. The local food pantry - the same one Dorian had been stocking with donations, the one feeding families who had nowhere else to turn — was asking for financial assistance. Rising electricity costs had become a real concern. Without help, the lights could go out on the very place so many depended on.

And then, in the comments, someone tagged *D-Max Merch*. Not a business. Not a nonprofit. Not a grant organization. A kid.

Someone in the community looked at a crisis - a real, urgent, adult problem - and thought of a child as the answer. That moment deserves to sit with you for a second. Because it says everything about what Dorian had built and who he had become in the eyes of the people around him. He wasn't seen as a child doing cute things for a good cause. He was seen as someone who could actually move the needle. Someone worth calling on when it mattered.

I showed Dorian the post. He smiled and gave a small

nod - the kind that says, I've got this. Someone had seen him as part of the solution. I could almost see the shift happening in real time - from being tagged in a comment to taking full ownership of the mission.

He didn't hesitate. He set a new goal: cover two months of the pantry's electricity costs.

The idea spread quickly. A local natural grocery store wanted in. A hot cocoa stand popped up. Word traveled. Dorian shared the mission, made the need visible, and little by little, money started flowing toward the pantry. Each week he walked through the door carrying envelopes of cash donation - and the relief on their faces when he arrived said more than any thank-you ever could.

When we stopped by after the holidays, the space looked different. Really different. The kind of different that stops you in the doorway.

Donations filled the room floor to ceiling. And then I noticed the extra shelves - the ones that had sat empty for so long they had almost become part of the background, easy to overlook, a quiet reminder of what wasn't there. They were full. Every single one of them.

It took a moment to absorb. This wasn't just a well-stocked pantry. This was what change looks like when it's standing right in front of you. The manager paused, looked around, and said she couldn't remember the last time they'd had this many supplies.

Standing there, watching it unfold, I realized something else was happening beneath the generosity. This wasn't just about one fundraiser or one kid showing up. It was a pattern revealing itself in real time. When a need becomes visible, people don't just respond - they organize and momentum builds. This is what systems thinking actually looks like in a community. Start noticing what's breaking, what keeps resurfacing, and how people are already willing to step forward when they feel connected to the outcome. There's a line from Designing Your Life by Bill Burnett and Dave Evans that captures this perfectly: *"You don't have to have it all figured out for the rest of your life; you just have to create the compass for what life is about for you right now."* That's exactly what Dorian did. Faced with a real, immediate need, he didn't try to solve everything. He set direction. He focused on what mattered in that moment and invited others to lead with him. Leadership doesn't always look like having all the answers- sometimes it's just noticing what's in front of you, choosing a direction, and making it easy for others to join in. When you name the need, set a goal, and open the door for collaboration, momentum has a way of building itself.

Once people begin to feel that momentum, imagination tends to widen. One night, Dorian had a friend over, and we were talking about the teddy bear drive idea around the kitchen table. What started as a simple conversation turned electric. His friend leaned forward, eyes bright, and began naming restaurants and local businesses-places he knew would care, places across the country. He was thinking BIG. He wasn't asking if it could work. He was imagining how far it could go. I felt myself getting swept up right alongside them. Their excitement was contagious-ideas stacking on ideas, momentum building in real time. Watching their minds light up like that is always incredible. Then we paused. I reminded them, and myself, that leadership isn't just about dreaming big. It's about pacing the dream. We talked about starting with the original goal. Testing it. Seeing how it worked. Working out the systems before scaling. This did not need to become a multi-state teddy bear drive yet.

Urgency often arrives the moment people glimpse potential, and resisting that pull takes discipline. Sustainable leadership is rarely built through speed alone. It is built through rhythm - the willingness to keep showing up after the excitement settles, to pace the work, check alignment, and make sure what is being built still fits the life surrounding it. The dream matters and so does learning how to carry it well.

What the Room Actually Held

After we published *D-Max's Birthday Wish*, everything seemed to pick up speed at once. One moment we were celebrating the launch, the next we were traveling, showing up for games, stepping back into school routines, and juggling calendars that didn't leave much space to pause. Instead of slowing down, we leaned into the momentum and planned an event that brought it all together: a book launch and a Birthday Cake Fundraiser in one. Dorian had his own criteria. It had to include: a DJ, basketball, cupcakes, and a place where kids could move, laugh, and just have fun together. We promoted it everywhere. Radio. Local news. Flyers sent home with kids at school. In my mind, all that motion meant the room would be full. Instead, it was quiet. I stood there, taking it in, and felt that familiar tightening in my chest. The unspoken question rose immediately: *Did we get this wrong*? When I zoomed out, the answer became clearer. We hadn't failed-we had confused the invitation. People didn't know which part of themselves the event was for. Was it a fundraiser? A celebration? A kids' party? In an ideal world, each piece would have had its own moment, its own audience. It was a lesson I was still digesting when I looked at Dorian. He was having the time of his life. He was on the basketball court, playing game after game with his dad, his stepdad, and his best friend-music blasting, laughter echoing off the walls. DJ Sparkles had brought Vinny, the cat with her, Dorian's absolute favorite, and at that point the party was officially complete. He was happy. Fully present. Unbothered by the low attendance.

I stood there watching him, holding both things at once-the disappointment I felt as a mom and the joy I was witnessing as a parent. That's when I realized something uncomfortable and important: he didn't see the low attendance as a reflection of his worth. In that moment, I did. He wasn't counting people. He wasn't questioning himself. He wasn't shrinking. He was playing, laughing, connecting-exactly as he always does. That's when I understood that I had something to learn from him.

We collected donations. We sold a few books. Most importantly, we had fun. That event didn't just change how I thought about success - it changed how I learned to lead alongside him.

Meeting Him Where He Was

For a long time, Dorian and I talked about writing a children's book based on his adventures. I could see it clearly - the lessons, the potential, the impact it could have on other kids. We met with children's book authors, gathered advice, and talked through what it might become.

On paper, it all looked simple.

But creative work is rarely linear, especially when the person holding the story cannot yet see it the way you do.

Dorian did not know where to begin. The idea felt too big, too abstract, too undefined. What looked clear to me felt overwhelming to him.

That was the first lesson: vision does not transfer simply because you explain it well.

Instead of pushing harder at the kitchen table, I realized I needed to meet him where his thinking naturally opened - on the basketball court.

Moving. Shooting hoops. Talking without the pressure of writing anything down.

I asked simple questions. At first, the answers were short. A word here, a shrug there, an occasional clarifying thought or small idea he wanted to explore.

Then something shifted.

The rhythm of movement made space for thought. Ideas started flowing. Energy changed. What had felt like resistance began turning into ownership. That moment mattered because it reinforced something I have seen repeatedly: when people struggle to engage, the answer is not always more pressure. Often, it is a different entry point.

Dorian and my mother later worked through page layout, flow, and edits together, and it was powerful to watch them side by side shaping the story.

After the book was published, Dorian initially pushed the title of "author" back toward me. Over time, he began claiming it in his own way - still generous with credit, but clearer about the role he had played.

He had to grow into it and that growth could not be rushed.

What this process reinforced for me is something leadership keeps teaching in different forms: moving a vision forward does not always begin by asking someone to step into your way of thinking. Sometimes it begins by understanding where their own thinking is most alive and building from there.

Real leadership often looks less like directing and more like adjusting the conditions until ownership becomes possible.

The Story Isn't Over

I have to finish this book, not because the stories are finished, but because no meaningful life ever arrives fully complete on the page. There are more stories. More moments. More proof that the *D-Max Effect* is still unfolding in real time - in ordinary conversations, unexpected acts of courage, and the ways people choose to show up for one another every day. I know that will continue long after this final page.

Endings are rarely about saying everything. More often, they are about knowing when something has been carried far enough to place into someone else's hands. That understanding feels personal because my father taught so much without ever needing long explanations. His lessons were steady, practical and they lasted. I wish he were here to hold this book. To see how what he modeled kept moving forward. To recognize his influence not only in me, but in the way his grandson now leads - with steadiness, warmth, and a natural instinct to notice others.

His absence has sharpened my relationship with time. So has losing others I loved, including Eliza, whose courage made life feel both fragile and deeply urgent in ways I still carry. Time clarifies what matters. Not everything important should wait for a perfect season, a clearer plan, or a less complicated moment. Some things need to be said while they are still alive in us. Some things need to be finished while they are still imperfect. Everything in these pages points to one simple truth: the *D-Max Effect* was never meant to stay inside one family, one child, or one community. It is what happens when potential is noticed early, trust is extended generously, and people are invited into meaningful work before they feel fully ready. It is not fast, not flashy, and often unnoticed at first but it lasts.

It begins when we notice potential early, invite people - especially children - into meaningful work, model integrity and kindness consistently, build alongside others rather than above them, and let recognition remain a by-product rather than the goal. It is not fast. It is rarely flashy. It often goes unnoticed at first. But it lasts.

Recently, Dorian received a package in the mail.

Inside were fifteen handwritten notes from second graders - children he had visited months earlier. They wrote about his book, their favorite sports, their pets, their favorite colors, and how much it meant that someone had come just to spend time with them. One note read: *"You are the youngest author I now."* The misspelling did not matter. What mattered was that someone took the time to write it - honestly, imperfectly, and - with care. That is the kind of return most meaningful work leaves behind: proof that presence stayed with someone after you were gone.

That is where this story pauses, though I hope the conversation continues. If these pages stay with you, I hope you will notice where the *D-Max Effect* appears in your own world and one day share where it led, because meaningful work rarely ends when a book does. It keeps moving through the people willing to carry it forward.

The D-Max Effect

Your Turn

Think of a moment when you let a child see you navigate your own emotions honestly. What did that teach them that words couldn't?

What would your community look like if one more adult decided to say: I see this. I believe in it and I can help?

Who in your community - a coach, a neighbor, a teacher-has shown up the way Dorian's partners did? Have you told them what that meant?

What is the version of the *D-Max Effect* that only you can create with the skills, relationships, and resources you already have?

About the Author

Lisa Liberatore is the entrepreneur, author, and systems builder who has spent her career proving that the most powerful resources aren't found in boardrooms - they're found in relationships, lived experience, and the untapped potential of young people.

A multi-business founder and author of the **Power of Transparency,** Lisa has built movements at the intersection of business, community, and youth leadership. She is the architect of frameworks that don't just inspire - they work.

But her most important role? Mom.

It was watching her son Dorian navigate the world that sparked **The D-Max Effect** - a groundbreaking framework revealing exactly how confidence, belonging, and true leadership are ignited when young people are trusted with real responsibility. This isn't theory. This is lived, proven, and transformational.

Lisa is the rare voice who brings together education, business, philanthropy, and civic leadership into something that creates immediate impact and changes the trajectory of what's possible.

If you've ever believed young people are capable of more - this book will show you how to prove it.

The D-Max Effect

www.ingramcontent.com/pod-product-compliance
Lightning Source LLC
Chambersburg PA
CBHW050006070726
47592CB00018B/1061